Aliens

With thanks to Gerd for exclusive cover image
geralt/Gerd Altmann/pixabay.com

ISBN-9798536930779

Aliens

The Alien Agenda

By
Brian Hunter

Published by
Wizard Way
Rainbow Wisdom
Ireland

ABOUT THE AUTHOR

Brian Hunter is an American author and Life Coach based in Los Angeles, California. Brian is the author of *Evolve, The Hunter Equation, Heal Me, Rising To Greatness, The Walk-In,* and *Aliens.* His books have sold around the world and have been Best Sellers within their genres. Brian was acknowledged as being intuitive as a child, and then later in life was attributed as having psychic abilities, as chronicled in his dramatic memoir *The Walk-In.* Brian was once listed as one of the top 50 psychics in the world. Brian has worked with people from all over the world, including celebrities and captains of industry. Brian was an original cast member of the TV series pilot "Missing Peace," in which psychics worked with detectives to solve cold cases. He has also worked as an actor and model in Hollywood, and been featured in various movie and TV productions. Brian's current focus is on his writing and life coaching work, helping clients from all walks of life.

www.brianhunterhelps.com

DEDICATION

I dedicate this book to my social media family who inspired me and encouraged me to write this book. You asked for it, so here it is. Also dedicated to those who support me through their contributions as clients and benefactors, so that I may continue with my work.

CONTENTS

CHAPTER ONE
The Abduction

I do not like to talk about it. It makes me feel embarrassed, stupid, and crazy. I have done a good enough job of embarrassing myself and making myself look crazy as it is. If you have read my memoir *The Walk-In,* you know what I am talking about. But for those who have not, I have aired my dirty laundry for all to see, and humiliated myself in the hope that it might help others. Oh, and I have been a professional psychic. So even on a good day, my tinfoil hat is always bright and shiny for everyone to see.

I feel ridiculous sometimes. Embarrassed. Even ashamed. I know my family thinks I am nuts. But I'm not. I am a professional Life Coach and I help people with very complex and difficult problems. I have also managed to write multiple self-help books that have done very well. I am very sane, boring, organized, analytical, and even a skeptical person. I tend not to believe in most conspiracy theories, and I always rely on logic before intuition. So even the "psychic camp" won't have me because I am not "all in." I prefer to stay grounded and always consult established facts and science first when they are available.

I grew up poor and I worked hard mowing lawns and getting straight A's in school. I was a strait-laced kid who never drank, never smoked, never did drugs, and never went to parties. I was a nerd who was also very much an outdoors guy connected to nature. I never lied and I always kept my word. I had my share of tragedies starting at a very young age, but I had no history of mental illness. In fact, I was the "rock" that others came to with their problems, even at a very young age.

But then later in my life, the shit hit the fan. I had some things happen to me that I never talked about. Then I had even more things happen to me after that. Tragedies and nothing but problems piled onto each other. These things changed me from a skeptical cynical machine-like businessperson, into the tinfoil-hat-wearing-person I am today.

With that said, I like what I do. I help people. I even save people. I make a difference. It is meaningful. But I am still that orderly and proud person deep inside that does not like to be looked at as crazy.

So why would I want to discuss more outrageous things that would make people think I am even more crazy and ridiculous than they currently think I am? The answer is simple. First, it is the right time to do it. It is time we all talk about it more openly. Secondly, I believe that many others are in the same boat as myself. It is time we stop this stigma surrounding "aliens," "UFOs," and "abductions."

Many of you reading this have had your own experiences. Perhaps you have been afraid to say something, or perhaps you said something and now others think you are nuts. I don't know about you, but I am tired of my own experiences and feelings being victimized by society saying they are invalid, lies, wrong, crazy, or stupid.

It is time people evolved into living closer to their own truths. This means owning your own experiences, feelings, and beliefs. Yes, there will be trolls who make fun of you, or try to make you feel invalid as a person. But it has to start somewhere. If you won't stand up for yourself, then who will?

Thus, I throw myself to the wolves and maybe encourage others to also come forth with their experiences. I hope to shed some light on the topic of aliens, UFOs, abductions, and what this means for us as individuals and society.

This is an open topic book and discussion. I do not care if you disagree with my assumptions, assertions, theories, or the accounting of my own private experiences. This book is not about me. This book is about empowering everyone out there having similar experiences, and what these mean for each of us individually, as well as society and humanity. So never mind me. I urge you to jump into this book yourself with your own experiences, opinions, and theories. Perhaps use my thoughts to test or amplify your own thoughts. Let's talk about it. Let's have a discussion. I will go first. Here is what happened to me.

I used to live in a large house on the edge of a freshwater lake. It was a very rural area. It would be busy in the summer with others staying at their seasonal cottages, but during the late Fall and Winter, I would be one of the only people living in the area. My home was one of only two year-round homes on the entire road. In fact, there were not very many year-round homes in that entire area of the lake. In the winter you had a feeling that you were truly alone and isolated, and indeed you were.

Many people commented that they would feel too creeped-out and scared to live in that kind of isolation there. Certainly, if there were ever a problem, it would take maybe an hour for police to arrive, for example. So those of us who lived out there in the off-season were truly on our own.

I enjoyed the isolation and quiet. I worked all day in town about a half hour from my house. At that time, I owned a very successful real estate services company. I would go into my offices inside a bank building dressed in a suit and be very focused all day with my responsibilities. I think most viewed me as a very "all-business" kind of guy. I usually kept a professional distance from those who worked under me, and I always had to maintain a strong level of professionalism and respect. I was not someone who ever "let their hair down" in front of employees or clients.

When I would come home in the evening, I would get into some comfortable clothes, eat my dinner while I watched the news, then I would retire to my master bedroom upstairs, where I would watch one

11

or two TV shows in bed before "lights out." It was a very boring existence really, but during the winter I just focused on work and had no social or home life.

I always slept very well, and then would wake up early to do it all over again the next day. I did not need any sleeping aids to fall asleep, I slept with the lights off, and I was not on any medications. Usually my nights sleeping were non-eventful, and I would not even get up to use the bathroom at any point during the night. I would just sleep right through. That is until one particular night.

As usual for wintertime there, I went to bed early, between 8:30PM and 9:00PM. On this particular evening, I was feeling fine, was not ill, and nothing unusual was going on with me at the time. I think I must have fallen asleep fairly quickly. However, the next thing I remember after turning the TV and lights off, was waking up, opening my eyes, and seeing a HUGE bright flash of light outside my large picture window of my bedroom that looked out onto the lake.

My bedroom was maybe about thirty feet or so from the water's edge. From the edge of the house, there was a deck, and then between the deck and the water was a small beach. My bedroom window only looked out onto this beach and the lake. There were no other cottages, roads, or driveways adjacent to that window. On the other side of the lake there were no roads or cottages at all. Basically, there was no possible source of headlights to shine inside my window from that perspective and location. Thus, I had never seen any lights, especially bright lights from looking out that window. It would not be possible unless there was something on the lake. The lake had ice on it at the time, but not thick enough to drive a vehicle on it.

Also, I had never seen a light like this before. It was huge and blinding. It would have had to be a very large and powerful spotlight, more powerful than anything I had experienced before in my life. It was very momentary, and if I had opened my eyes a second later, I might have missed it. But I distinctly remembered opening my eyes

12

and seeing this incredible flash of light. I think I may have felt a bit disoriented by it as well.

Startled by this split-second flash of light, I sat up and glanced at the digital alarm clock on my nightstand. It was 10:02PM. This was actually shocking to me. Judging by how I felt, I was expecting the clock to say 5:00AM or something like that. I felt like I had been sleeping all night. Despite my sleep being interrupted by waking up to this flash of light, I felt fully rested, and surely it must be morning and almost time for my alarm to go off to start another day.

How could the clock be indicating that I had only been sleeping for about one hour? How could I feel so fully rested after only one hour of sleep? It was as if I was caught in some weird time warp. I sat up in bed very confused. I was somewhat disoriented, trying to figure out what the huge flash of light coming from the lake was, and why I felt like I had been sleeping all night, but had only been sleeping for one hour.

My business-like logical mind could not process or resolve what had just happened. Therefore, my mind set it aside and I ended up settling back down and falling asleep. I woke up at my normal time in the morning when my alarm clock went off. I felt normal, but immediately started thinking about what happened.

When I got out of bed and walked into the bathroom, I noticed something on my thumb that caught my eye. I turned the light on to make it even brighter than the early morning sun and took a closer look. There appeared to be a fresh puncture wound or mark on the side of my thumb. It was on my right thumb and appeared as if it was a tiny needle puncture wound with no blood. It was a very tiny red spot, and I could actually see there was a tiny hole on the side of my thumb. But it was not bleeding and there was no dried blood or evidence of anything else around this hole or on my thumb.

I remember staring at it and trying to look at it from different angles. I tried to think of what could have caused it. I really had no explanation. I had not injured my thumb or hand at all the prior day, or that night. I had not cut my nails or done anything like that either. Additionally, the wound was something I had never seen before. How odd to see such a tiny puncture wound on a thumb with no evidence of bleeding, even though it looked like it should have bled.

I briefly looked myself over, as if I were counting my fingers and toes to make sure everything was still there, and I saw nothing else odd about myself. I also felt fine and normal, although I knew it had been an odd night of sleep and I was confused and disoriented about what had happened.

I looked outside my bedroom window just to see if there was anything unusual. Nothing was out there. The ice was still covering the lake. The only odd thing was perhaps that it looked as if some of the light snow covering the lake had melted in front of my house during the night. But the ice itself was still there and solid. Nothing had broken through the ice. Nothing had been on my beach.

It was a work day and I had to transition my mind back to getting ready for work and leaving the house. On my drive to the office, I decided not to mention my story to anyone at the office. I felt like I was always being judged for whether or not I had all my marbles intact, and whether I was professional enough to handle important responsibilities. I might have been the boss, but I was also working with bank executives, business partners, clients, and my accountant. Any sign of instability from me would be bad for business. Therefore, I decided to keep my little story to myself and brush it under the rug in my own head so that I could focus on the normal business at hand.

However, since then, off and on, I have revisited this incident in my mind hoping to remember something that had happened, or come to some theories on what exactly happened. Obviously, it goes without saying that I concluded it was supernatural. But what kind of supernatural event? Did an event take place inside my bedroom, and

14

I never left my bedroom? Or did an event take place outside on a "craft" hovering over the lake? Or was I zapped out of my bedroom and into something else or somewhere else?

I can tell you with fair certainty that I did not walk out of my house under my own power, or even with the assistance of others. I was sleeping in underwear, my outside door was way on the opposite end of the house on the floor below me, and it was wintertime and very cold outside. My door had remained locked. So I know I didn't leave through my door out into the cold outside wearing nothing but underwear.

I also felt that nobody and nothing had been inside my bedroom other than me. I cannot prove this, but I have always been intuitive, even before my psychic abilities came in strong. I am pretty well convinced that my bedroom had not been invaded.

That leaves us with the more likely possibility that I had been "zapped out" of my bedroom through the walls or roof or whatever, and then zapped back inside the same way.

The only other possibility is that there was some trick of consciousness or remote examinations done to me while I remained in my bedroom, but without any other "beings" having to actually be in my bedroom with me. But how can this happen when something created a puncture wound on my thumb? Additionally, let's pretend that I was just a crazy delusional lunatic that particular night and nothing happened at all. If that is true, then again, how did I get the puncture wound on my thumb? What was the flash of light? What explains the weird time warp sensation of having slept all night when I was only sleeping for one hour?

I know I am asking all the questions, and some of you might be hoping this book would be providing all of the answers rather than questions. We will get there if we can. I just think it is important to examine this in a transparent, clear, objective, and orderly fashion. All I can do is offer my experience as "evidence" of what happened to me. We can work together to figure out the possibilities and explanations. I am not trying to convince anyone of anything, nor do I have an agenda to prove one theory over another theory. My agenda, if I have one, is simply to be one more person who can provide information or evidence to show that these supernatural things are indeed happening. It's real, and just dismissing people as crazy is no longer a legitimate response.

In addition to examining the situation and myself from a physical perspective, I also did some contemplating mentally and emotionally. I tried to remember, sense, or feel anything that I might have experienced that night. My conclusion was that whatever it was, I was not afraid. I felt I had cooperated and did not feel under threat at any time. There was something "familiar" about the experience that I have been unable to put my finger on. But it was as if I had done it before, or that I knew those who had perpetrated the "operation."

I felt others had also been abducted and seemed scared, but for some reason I was not scared. I did not feel traumatized in any way. I felt as if I had been treated "professionally." I did not feel any pain physically or mentally. I also felt it would happen again.

And it did. Off and on for a couple years, I would wake up with a weird feeling, and would have a fresh puncture wound on my thumb. But that was it. Never again did I see a flash of light or have the weird time warp sensation. It was just the thumb. It became an amusing thing I would notice when it happened, and I would think, "They got me again last night," but then I would proceed with my day. Eventually, the puncture wounds would never appear again, and after some years I moved from that property.

I never spoke of my experiences until my life drastically had changed and I was no longer a business professional. The first time I even mentioned it was when I published my first book, *The Hunter Equation*. I mentioned it again in my book *The Walk-In*. By then, I had a nice shiny tinfoil hat on my head, and it seemed appropriate and

16

relevant to share my experiences. However, it would also lead some to just assume I had lost my mind and was delusional and crazy.

Yes, it is true I had some traumatic events and life changes later on, BUT it cannot be ignored that my "abduction?" experience took place long before any traumatic events, and happened while I was a very stable, cynical, skeptical, business-minded professional person with little interest in the paranormal.

Notice I have avoided using the phrase "alien abduction," or just "abduction" until closer to the end of my testimony. I want our examination of aliens, UFOs, and abductions, to be done in a very sane and orderly way without jumping to conclusions for the sake of being dramatic. My own experiences and your experiences will serve as a basis for our discussions going forward, but they are only pieces of evidence, and not the only story, and not the full story. So, let us all keep very open minds while not automatically jumping to dramatic conclusions. With that said, I am afraid to say that this possible abduction incident I just described is not the only paranormal event I have to offer for consideration. As if I don't sound crazy enough after this, I have an even crazier story to tell next.

CHAPTER TWO
The Walk-In

It is difficult enough to say publicly that you may have been abducted by aliens. However, it is even more difficult for me to discuss this next incident. This incident was the defining moment of my life. At the time it felt as if it had scrambled my brains, and it caused mental and emotional trauma and damage that lasted for years.

I never discuss this incident with anyone in person. I don't want to talk about it. It's very personal and private to me, and also filled with pain. It was a secret I kept until I had the courage to publish my memoir and third book, *The Walk-In*. I chronicled this incident in one chapter of that book. I will provide an accounting of that event again in this book because I believe it is very much related to our discussion of aliens, as you will eventually realize. If you have already read *The Walk-In* and are very familiar with the event, you might decide to skip this chapter, as it is a repost of what you already read. Conversely, if you have not read *The Walk-In*, and would like a wider view of what happened to me, along with all background details, then you might consider reading *The Walk-In*.

I tried to think of a way to avoid including this incident within this book, but it would be unfair to you and the book, because in order for me to provide a new perspective on the subject of aliens, I absolutely have to talk about this incident. Our examination of aliens is going to broaden to a psychological and metaphysical discussion later on as we develop more advanced ideas about aliens than what is currently out there in the general genre of aliens.

I need to preface this event first, so that you can better understand what happened. What I am about to describe to you is a phenomenon called a "walk-in." A walk-in is when a foreign consciousness or soul from another person or entity, enters your body and mind, to either co-exist with your present consciousness, or even partially displace it. Obviously, this is a phenomenon that cannot be proven at this point, and thus you will hear different definitions and opinions based upon who you ask. The general idea is that the consciousness or soul of a deceased person is able to enter into a living person and continue to exist as it did before. The recipient of the walk-in will essentially have two consciousnesses or souls within them, and there will be a process of assimilating the two together, or one will become more submissive while the other plays a more dominant role. The recipient of a walk-in will have definite changes to their personality and intellectual ability since they now have access to the additional new consciousness within them. This can clearly cause mental health problems as well, especially in the beginning after the walk-in event. It is believed by many that a walk-in can only happen if the recipient INVITES the other consciousness into them. Obviously, most people do not, and would not, do this. This is thought to be a rare phenomenon, but many people have begun to come forward believing they have had this happen to them. It sounds totally crazy, but to those it has happened to, it is all too terrifying and real. It is one of those things that can be almost impossible to understand if you have never experienced it, but is absolutely clear to those who have.

In this chapter I am not going to fully go into the entire background of what led up to the walk-in, or all the very personal matters involved. This particular book is not about me. If you feel you want the broader and more personal story, you can find it in my book *The Walk-In*. For our purposes here, we are going to stick to the incident itself so that we can add it to our pile of evidence that will be used in the broader and more detailed discussions to come later in this book. With that said, I need to provide enough background information so that you can fully understand the person or entity in question that would become "the walk-in entity." Therefore, please bear with me as I have to provide adequate information and context of what led up to the event, and why it is so important for you to understand who the "walk-in entity was and is."

Just to be clear, this incident happened many years after the abduction event. My life was in decline in the sense that I was in the process of losing my business, relationships, my home, and in general was in a very bad place in my life. It is safe to say I was very traumatized and emotionally hurt. But with that said, I want to make it clear that I had never engaged in any activities such as drugs, drinking, smoking, or anything mind-altering. I was depressed, but I was not on any medication at all. I was certainly quite sane, and other than depression, I was not suffering from any mental illness, nor had I ever had a history of mental illness.

It all started one day when I was randomly befriended by a stranger. Chaz first approached me on social media. He was very forward and confident as if he already knew me. It was very strange. I was very standoffish and nervous at first. I resisted his contact initially, thinking he was just some crazy person on social media. However, even in very short messaging conversations, he seemed so intelligent and interesting, that I was very intrigued. It was like a mystery, and I wanted to know more. I was lonely, scared, sad, depressed, and seeking some kind of guidance, help, or comfort in my life. Why not talk to Chaz. What could be the harm in that? What could possibly go wrong? Well, it was not long at all before Chaz said he much preferred to talk on the phone so he knew whom he was really dealing with. He asked if it was okay if he called me. I was again very nervous and hesitated. But his confidence and seeming intelligence was so intriguing, I could not help myself, so I agreed.

Ten minutes later my phone rings, and it is a very nice and normal sounding young man on the phone. He was so at ease, it was kind of contagious, and I very quickly felt at ease myself. He asked me all kinds

20

of questions. In retrospect, most people would have advised not to give any personal info away to a stranger like this, but I sang like a bird. I told him about where I lived, my business I had back east, how I was struggling, and so on. Totally crazy. He was clearly interviewing or interrogating me, and I was fully cooperating. He was so nice, and I think I was loving the attention and attentive interaction. Most of all though, I was blown away by his unusually high level of intelligence. He was so well spoken and seemed to always know exactly what to say, and he knew something about every topic that would come up in discussion. I had never really come across this before and I found it odd and refreshing. We clicked immediately and got along amazingly well. I felt connected and comfortable with him in minutes. Was this guy even human? I had never come across a person like this before, and my first impression was that he was not anything close to a normal human being.

These phone conversations went on every day for a few weeks. I loved talking to him. He was such good company and I soon realized he appreciated my company as well. Somehow I was able to learn a couple things about him despite his demeanour of secrecy, but not much. I learned he was gay. He did not *sound* gay at all, but he mentioned how he was usually attracted to young guys. This is relevant because it is important to note here that I was significantly older than Chaz, so I would not have been a "younger guy" that he would have preferred "in that way."

He had a brother who seemed to be a huge part of his life, since every other sentence included "Martin this" and "Martin that." He had done lots of traveling and had been all over the world. He loved watching TV documentaries about any subject, but especially history and the paranormal. He was especially fascinated with spiritual powers, psychic ability, and ghosts. One thing I would have assumed he would be interested in, but he actually felt uncomfortable discussing, was anything to do with alien life and UFOs. Whenever I

21

mentioned aliens or UFOs, I could feel his energy constrict, and he would pause or stumble and change the subject. I thought this was weird for a guy who loved all other topics of the paranormal.

He shared with me that his family felt he was highly psychic and they often called him "the alien" (a name he didn't like), because he always knew everything about many subjects, and acted differently than most humans. He told stories about how he could predict what people were thinking and what actions people would take. He told stories about his brother taking him to casinos, and he would correctly choose numbers on the roulette reel.

I found Chaz's comments on religion particularly interesting. Chaz said he was not religious, and actually resented the control that religion played in people's lives. But at the same time, he was intensely spiritual. He spoke many times of how close he felt to God. I could tell he had a very personal and valued relationship with God. Chaz had done in-depth research on Jesus from an archaeological and historical perspective. He had explained to me how he felt the real birth of Jesus would have been in the spring.

Chaz also seemed to be very well versed in Greek Mythology. He was fascinated with Atlantis, the Bermuda Triangle, and many such things. The topic of aliens would come up during the discussion of Atlantis, and although he clearly believed aliens were real and existed, he once again seemed uncomfortable talking about them, as I mentioned earlier. I think maybe it hit too close to home since his family and friends were constantly accusing him of being one.

One interesting conversation we had though, was him telling me about a time he had to go to a "secret installation" with his father. He said they kept things there that nobody thinks exist, and that nobody has any idea what is really going on in this world. He also said it was located in a place that would surprise me. At the time, I interpreted the topic was involving aliens, but it could have been military or technology based also. I really have no idea. He did say that he, Chaz,

22

had invented something once that solved a problem "they" were having, but he did not say anymore. He said it is always the simple solutions that work best, meaning that what he did was so simple, that others there were embarrassed they did not come up with it first. Mostly when talking to Chaz, I just listened in silence, wonderment, and confusion.

We also talked about the fact I loved hunting when I was younger. I excitedly told him how I loved hunting season every year, and had been successful at getting some nice trophies in my past. This information did not go over well, though. He shared with me how he could not stand the thought of killing an animal. A person maybe, but an animal, never. I laughed nervously and changed the subject.

It did not take long for me to feel a bit intimidated, and I was always afraid he would ask me something I knew nothing about. At the risk of sounding overly arrogant, this was the first time I had extended interactions with someone so completely more intelligent than I was. I was way over my head with Chaz. It was obvious to me he was a certified Genius. Thus, when he started talking about a topic, I would typically keep my mouth shut and just listen, unless he asked me a question.

However, he did seem very interested in my thoughts, and in me. He asked me many questions every conversation. There was one time he turned the tables on me and said, "So you were pre-med in school, own a business, have extensive knowledge of law, banking, and you do all your own accounting work?" I said, "Yes I guess that's right." There was a pause as if he was actually impressed for half a moment. Then he said, "You know, my dad always said that a family needs three things: a great doctor, a great lawyer, and a great accountant." I laughed and reminded him I was not *actually* a medical doctor or lawyer. He said, "Yes I know, but you have extensive knowledge in all three areas; do you know how rare that is for someone as young as you?" I did not reply and we changed subject, but I could tell he was interested, intrigued, and maybe 10% impressed.

Finally, one day, my curiosity got the better of me and I touched "the third rail" and asked if he wanted to meet up in person sometime. I could tell immediately from his reaction that I had just asked him to turn into a pretzel and crawl twenty miles through mud. I immediately backed off from my request because I did not want to scare him away or alienate him, since I really valued our conversations and did not want him to vanish.

However, a couple days later he brought up the subject himself. He asked if I still wanted to meet him in person. I said, "Yes absolutely." He paused. I even think he put me on hold for a moment. He came back and asked if I would come to Santa Monica. I said yes, no problem. He then said he would let me know in the next few days when and where exactly. Being used to his vague cryptic answers by now, I said yes, no problem. A day or so later he gave me the time and place, and asked me to make sure it was only me coming, and that I did not tell anyone my business of where and when I was meeting people. I said yeah of course.

Finally the day came. I was really nervous. But why was I nervous? I was only going to meet a casual friend, and I knew him really well by now so there should be no awkwardness. But something deep inside me knew it would be significant and epic.

I arrived at the specified location, which was a more remote than normal parking lot at the beach. I was dressed very casually and waited by my vehicle. Nobody was there except for several stray empty cars. I looked all around to see if I could see something or someone of note. Nothing. I waited. After ten minutes I started to get a sinking feeling that I had been stood up like an idiot. Just when I was starting to become annoyed, I noticed some interesting movement. I saw a big black shiny SUV drive in the lot followed by three cars, which all looked like those undercover police cars. They pulled off to the side of the parking lot near me. I just watched, not knowing what was

24

going on. Certainly it was not for me. Except it was. Two men in the first car behind the SUV got out first and approached the SUV. Then two more men from the other cars got out, but stood by their cars. The men, who approached the SUV opened the door to the SUV. Out slid who I knew immediately was Chaz. I had never seen a picture of Chaz, but I immediately sensed it was him. I could feel it in every bone in my body. I was totally shaking in my shoes at this point.

Out slid this young-looking guy with dark, perfect, short, specially styled hair, $1,000 sun glasses, some kind of $10,000 jacket, and shoes that must have been worth thousands to match. He was like a movie star combined with a royal prince. As he started walking toward me, the first two men came with him. As he grew closer, I got a closer look at him. He was a "10" on the looks scale, and the value of his sunglasses, clothes, and shoes doubled in value. I was frozen like a deer in front of 1,000 spotlights. Thank God he spoke first. He said "Hi Brian," and he shook my hand and gave me a hug. I said "Oh my god, Hi." Chaz responded by saying, "My name is not Oh My God, it's Chaz." I actually said "sorry" because I was not sure if he was being funny or if he was actually insulted. To this day I am still not sure. The two men looked inside my vehicle parked behind where I was standing, and they looked at me as if I was a possible terrorist, then they looked at Chaz, and Chaz nodded his head, and the men walked away back to their car and just stood there. I could not see how many people were in the SUV that carried Chaz, and nobody else ever came out.

I did not know what to do, so I let Chaz lead everything, including the conversation and where we would stand and talk. Chaz guided us a short distance closer to the beach so that we were not awkwardly talking in the parking lot. He said to me, "So are you nervous Brian?" I said "Yes, but it's okay, I'm fine." He then said, "Are you surprised?" I said yes. I told him he never said anything on the phone about "*this*", pointing to the security caravan. Chaz asked, "What is "*this?*" I again was not sure if he was insulted or not, and I said that I meant the

25

security people and all that. Chaz said, "Don't worry about them; just talk to me like we do on the phone." So I did. I talked to him normally from that moment on and never looked back. We talked for about an hour just like we had been doing on the phone for weeks. I began to feel totally at ease. We did not talk about anything of significance. I could tell the purpose of this encounter was not the conversation, but rather some kind of "inspection" or just "first meeting."

Eventually Chaz said he had to go. He said, "Well I better get going back to Malibu or my dad will kill me; he does not know I am here." Of course, I was thinking in my head, "how can nobody know where you are with a battalion of security following you." I was smart enough to keep my mouth shut this time. Chaz gave me a hug and said, "You know Brian, I knew I would like you; but I like you even more now after meeting you in person." He then walked back to the SUV. Security opened the door for him, he slid inside, and his caravan of four vehicles drove away. I stood there in the parking lot for maybe ten minutes stunned by what just happened.

Chaz and I resumed our regular daily phone conversations that would sometimes last hours. I think we both felt more comfortable and safe with each other; therefore, we both opened up more. He was very funny. Sometimes his humor could be dark and devilish, but always good natured toward me. I would ask him things like, "Do you always travel with that many security guards?", and he would laugh and say, "Of course not silly; I usually have twice that many, especially when I am with my family." He would go on to say that when the entire family travels out to dinner or any function together, they would usually have at least twelve "officers" and many cars.

I knew early on not to ask too many prying questions, but as time went on I was able to gracefully, at the right times and circumstances, ask him certain things. Over time I would learn that his step dad was a very important person high in the government. His mom worked for a very famous movie producer. They lived between two homes in

26

Malibu and San Francisco. He told me they could travel back and forth between the homes with no suitcase, and not even a toothbrush, because they had two of everything. Each house was totally equipped with everything they needed, including in their bathrooms and bedrooms.

Their "second home" was the Malibu house, which was a huge fancy beach house. His brother Martin apparently had a brand new white Lamborghini in the garage, which had plastic wrap around it to keep it safe; meaning he never drove it. Their primary home was in San Francisco in some ultra-exclusive gated neighborhood. The house sounded like some gigantic huge monstrosity of a mansion. Frankly, I had trouble even comprehending the level of wealth.

Chaz made it a point to discuss some of the practical and security measures they had. I think I was vetted enough at this point that he was being more open regarding such things. I kind of got the feeling that I was being groomed and prepared to deal with their "lifestyle situation" should we become closer friends. He would explain how they had a lockdown procedure at night where there would be "last call." "Last call" would be when you could go to the kitchen and get any drinks or food you wanted, before you had to be locked up in your room for the night. After last call and lockdown, you were stuck in your room. I am guessing they had motion detectors and such things in the hallways and stairways, and that is why nobody could leave their rooms. I asked what would happen if I accidentally left my room, and he said, "You might get shot." Then he laughed. Again, I was not sure if he was joking or not. They had "officers" that were stationed in the driveway and grounds all night. If anything odd was picked up on the sensors, the officers would go inside the house to check things (thus why I might be shot). Add to all this, two Doberman Pincher dogs which were basically set on "kill" mode, and you had to know the "secret word" to get the dogs to stand down.

Chaz and I discussed everything during our weeks and months of

27

phone conversations that seemed to last longer as time went on. It got to the point that I was on the phone with him for like half the day. I realized that my "function" at that time was to keep him company. I literally felt like maybe it was my "job," or perhaps this was an audition for a job, or maybe it was just nothing. He was actually quite lonely and isolated because he rarely went out and did things, due to all the security measures and his family's limitations on him. He spent most of his time reading and researching things. It turned out he was indeed a tested and certified Genius, and was always studying every subject known to man (and alien?). Chaz could answer any question you had about anything. Go ahead, try him. Whether it was about cooking, Hollywood, cars, computers, history, world issues, (insert list of all items on Wikipedia here).

I took advantage of this knowledge daily. I went to Chaz about all my business and financial questions, asking him all kinds of things and for advice. He provided me with good guidance I used daily. I came to totally depend on him. I depended on him for my emotional contact, my business advice, and hope for the future. Chaz in turn would tell me very personal things about him, and deep thoughts he had. Our conversations could be very random. One minute he would talk about cooking, and the next minute he would joke, he hoped he died young and beautiful in some fantastic fiery crash or something. One thing that always stuck with me is when he said to me, "You have had to work very hard for everything you have achieved, and have not had an easy life; it's time for that to change." The conversations would go back and forth similar to this on both sides. We had become very close, despite only meeting in person once. It felt as if we were best friends, but I looked up to him as a mentor also. However, in the background, I always felt as if I was being "interviewed" or evaluated for something.

Eventually, our conversations turned a little. They went away from random everyday things, to Chaz's ambitions and ideas. Chaz said he wanted to travel the world for a year, and visit various archaeological, spiritual, and mysterious landmarks. He hinted at the possibility of maybe me going with him. But just as quickly, he would start talking about working on an idea he had for a new type of car engine. The conversations would move in many different directions, and would always include questions to me about what I would do in certain scenarios, and what my feelings were about certain world problems. I always tried my best to answer "correctly," but always felt intimidated like my answers could not possibly ever be "correct enough."

Eventually, Chaz started talking about us meeting up again in person. However, this time it would be to meet his family. He suggested maybe Thanksgiving holiday since that was coming up. He said he would have to get his dad's approval and it was complicated. I totally understood. You see, Chaz had not yet told me the actual name/identity of his dad. What Chaz did not know is that I already knew who his stepdad was. Chaz, as smart as he was, had made one tiny slip-up previously about something. I, not exactly being an idiot, caught it. I did my own research and figured out who his stepdad was. His stepdad was indeed a very important government official.

I could not tell Chaz I had been stalking around and figured this out. I told Chaz I understood the complications, but that I would absolutely love to go up there for Thanksgiving. He asked how long I would want to stay, and I answered, "As long as you let me." We both laughed. He then indicated that if that went well, and I survived the encounter (joke?), that maybe I could join them for Christmas at their home in Canada.

Chaz warned me that if I came to their house I would have to face his dad and his brother, and it would not be easy. I nervously asked why. He said his dad would for sure interrogate me in his office. Chaz warned me to always be honest in all my answers to his dad, because his dad would only ask me questions to which he already knew the answers. He said his brother Martin would likely make it his mission

29

to have me feel as uncomfortable as possible, as a way of testing me, and initiation. Frankly, Chaz made a visit up there sound horrible. Looking back on this, I am not sure why I was so eager, but I think I sensed something amazing or important in the background.

It didn't take long before Chaz said he felt he almost had approval for my Thanksgiving trip, but first he had a trip he needed to take. I asked where. He said he had convinced his family to let him go to Oktoberfest in Germany. I asked how that works with his security. He said there would be no security, but he would be going with three of his closest friends (one of which I had heard about in detail already). He said his parents were very hesitant to let him go, but that he insisted and really wanted to do this. He asked me if it was okay he was doing this trip, since we would not be able to talk much while he was away. I was a bit surprised he was asking for my permission? I asked how long would he be gone, and he replied a week or two. He said we would not be able to talk every day, but that he would call me every three days for sure. I then told him I would go to my New England lake house and have some time at my house there. This is the same house where I had my previous suspected alien abduction incident. I still had this house even though I had moved to Los Angeles in between the two events I am describing.

I arrived back east at my New England lake house. Chaz was in Germany and I did not expect to hear from him for a few days. But the days started going by, and I never heard from Chaz. I started to become very concerned and on the fifth day I called his phone and left a voice mail. By the sixth day, I had a horrible feeling in my stomach that something terrible had happened and I started to become distraught. I knew I was being a bit irrational, but I was so certain of what I was feeling, as if there was a voice in my head telling me. On the seventh day, sometime around mid-morning, I walked into my home office to check my email. I saw an email from someone I did not know, but a name I recognized. It was the name of a person Chaz had described to me as "his best friend from childhood." His name was Jackson.

I very frantically opened the email. The email read,

"*Brian, this is Jackson, Chaz's friend. Martin has asked me to email you. It is with great sadness I have to tell you that Chaz was in a car accident in Germany and has passed away. I am very sorry to tell you this way, but I don't have your phone number. Feel free to email me if you want.*"

As I read it at first, time stopped. I think I was struck with lightning. I actually did not believe what I was seeing. I read it a second time. The second time, I felt my heart explode into thousands of pieces and drop into my stomach. Still in confusion, I read it a third time. The third time, it was like my head wanted to explode and I felt a strong painful tingle in my arms, chest, and up through my head. I felt as if I had been impaled by a huge metal rod. Feeling nothing but strong painful tingles, I saw black, and dropped to the floor. Out.

I don't know how long I was out for. When I came to, I was on the floor next to my desk with my face and eyes completely covered with a coating of dried tears. I remember I could not breathe very well; it was very labored and difficult. I immediately remembered why I was on the floor. I stayed on the floor motionless for a few minutes. It was as if I was paralyzed. Then I got up on my knees. I glanced at my computer and saw the email. I did not bother reading it again. I knew what it said. I stood up and had trouble keeping my balance at first. The tingling in my arms and chest was gone, but there was still some light tingling in my head. I felt like my heart had been removed. What I mean by this is that I felt dead inside. Actually, I felt dead period, like a zombie. My breathing continued to be very labored. All I could do is stand, or take some steps, then stop. My thoughts were very limited. I remember having to actually think and decide which direction I would walk in, as if it was a big decision and task. It also felt as if I had to actually *think* in order to breathe. It was as if I had to *decide* to breathe and think through each breath in order

31

for it to happen.

Honestly, it is hard for me to write my account of what happened at this point because I frankly do not remember much. I was in some kind of zombie daze and was completely brain dead and heart-dead. Only my labored breathing kept me alive, and that felt like it could quit at any moment. I remember that I was very concerned at how I was going to get back home to LA. I literally did not feel capable of driving to the airport; talking to ticket agents, navigating airports, and driving back home once in LA. The thought of all that was so overwhelming, it really seemed impossible to me. But I knew I had to somehow get home, and I somehow did, although I have very little memory of the trip home.

When I arrived back home in Los Angeles, I felt dead. I felt like a zombie. I was lost. I was sick. I did not think I could even feed myself. If that was not bad enough, what would happen next is even more confusing to me than what I already detailed. I think it was the next morning after arriving back home, and I was sitting in my office at my desk, where I would always have all my conversations with Chaz. I started to cry uncontrollably, which at the time felt random and odd to me. I am not sure if maybe it was because I was finally safe and secure back home, that maybe I felt I could "lose it." Well, I lost it alright. And everything changed. There was a sudden feeling of comfort out of nowhere. Well, actually it's not true it was coming from nowhere. It was coming from my right, meaning to the right of where I was. I felt a "presence", as if "it" was sitting next to me on my right, next to me behind my desk. I looked over to my right and saw something. It was like a light energy force. It was not a "ghost." It was more like normal air, except thicker. I recognized the energy as feeling like Chaz, like how he is, his energy, the feeling I get when talking to him or standing next to him. A couple seconds after that, I started getting messages (silent voices) in my head. The voice or message in my head was "yes it's me I'm here." I felt so calm and

32

comfortable in that moment. I started to cry again, but it was a different cry. This was more of a gentle cry of gratitude. I was so grateful and happy I was having this connection with Chaz. It was as if he was watching me, and waiting to connect. I mentally said to him, "I'm so relieved you are here, I missed you." For some reason, my next thoughts to him were "What's it like?" The voice in my head answered, "It was scary at first, but once I pushed off from my body, it did not hurt anymore." In my mind I was about to ask, "What's it like to be dead," but before I could even develop the entire thought and verbalize it in my head, the voice said, "I can't taste, smell, or feel anything; but I can go anywhere just by thinking it." Then I said, "I don't want you to leave." The voice in my head replied, "I can live on inside you if you want." I immediately said, "Yes, yes, yes," and I cried a little. The voice said, "Are you sure?" I said, "Yes absolutely, please, please, please," through gentle tears that were more out of exhaustion than mourning.

Then it hit! I felt a very strong and strange sensation go through me that made me shiver; the hair on my arms and neck stood up, and I had goose bumps. I felt a cool sensation, then a warm sensation. I think I almost passed out, but I know I did not. Then the energy that had been next to me on my right was gone. It was replaced by the sensation of a certain "presence" (or entity?) inside me. I went from feeling completely dead and empty inside, to having an actual life or presence inside me. The voice stopped speaking inside my head, and now I could *feel* the voice even though it was not speaking. I did not feel alone. I felt some "intelligence," or thing, or energy, actually inside my head. I became very tired as if all the previous days of drama and trauma had caught up to me finally, and I was going to faint. I went to bed.

I slept for maybe 16 hours. When I woke up, I felt very sick and foggy. I felt like there was literally a fog covering my eyes that I had trouble seeing through. I felt very tired. One thing I noticed is that I seemed to be breathing much better. But the improved breathing was replaced by an overwhelming tiredness.

Days went by, one by one, where it was the same routine. I would sleep all night. In the morning, I would wake up and use all my effort to get out of bed. I would use the bathroom, check my email, walk out to the dining area and look outside, and then I would feel very tired and need to go back to bed. I would lie in bed. Sometimes I would sleep, and sometimes I would just lay there. Then I might get up and use the bathroom, and rinse and repeat. I would say there was a very long sleep each night, then a series of six or so naps during the day, while the rest of the day was filled with sitting or resting.

Not too many days went by until I was starting to run out of cans of vegetable soup I had been eating. Vegetable soup and toast was all that I was eating. I had already lost some weight that I did not need to lose. I decided it was time to try and go outside, and walk down to my usual take-out restaurants and get a good lunch. I usually alternated my lunches between pizza and Mexican.

I got myself dressed in sweat pants and a t-shirt. I know my hair was a horrible mess so I wiped water on it. I walked down my exterior apartment stairs looking like I had been sleeping for days. Well, I had been sleeping for days, so okay. I walked down the sidewalk and I recall being careful to place my feet and steps one in front of the other because I felt it was possible I could fall. When I got down the street a bit where there were lots of other people, I started to experience some weird sensations. I noticed every time I looked at someone walking by me, I could sense what they were thinking and feeling. I was picking up on all kinds of random meaningless thoughts of each person walking past me. It was actually disconcerting for me. It was like constant noise coming at me that would not stop.

The second thing I noticed is that nobody was looking at me. I was looking at everyone, but everyone was looking straight ahead as if I was not there. I began to feel like I was not there. I felt invisible. I

34

started to get scared. I wondered, "Was I dead?" Maybe I died when I collapsed back east, and now I have been a ghost all this time? I thought it through, and other than the airport, I did not have any contact with people, and certainly no people who actually knew me personally. So I started to test the theory, and I remember waving and saying Hi to some lady walking by me. She ignored me as if I was not even there. I went into the takeout restaurant; nervous they would not see me and give me my food. I stood in line, still invisible, and feeling invisible, but when I got to the front of the line, they seemed to recognize that I was a person, and they gave me my food. I was very relieved. I went home as quickly as I could while still hearing all the thoughts of people passing by me. I got inside my apartment and was so glad to be back home inside, and gratified to have real food. I ate like I had not eaten in a month. I should have ordered three of those Mexican lunches.

I asked the inner voice if I was dead. There was no reply. I asked why I could sense what people are thinking. I did get a reply to that. It said, "There are many things you can do which you don't realize yet." My existing psychic abilities, which I had shown evidence of since a young boy, had just increased exponentially.

That was not all. I noticed I knew things I did not know before. I felt smarter in a way. It was a weird sensation, because I felt retarded in terms of thought function due to the "fog," but I felt I had volumes of data and information in my head that I did not have before. I was in a situation where I had to think carefully how I would take the garbage out, but if you asked me a question about anything else, I would have the information to answer it.

Most disconcerting, is that I also noticed my personality seemed different. I felt more laid back, relaxed, and funny. I felt like I was more interested in people now, whereas before I was more interested in business and money. I was now more interested in the journey, rather than in the destination like I had always focused on since a kid. I

35

had lost all interest in hunting, and just the thought of killing an animal was alarming to me. I found myself with a new interest in history, and viewing documentaries to learn new things. There were so many things where I felt I was a different person. Maybe the old Brian DID actually die?

One of the biggest changes for me was an overwhelming intense sense of spirituality. Previously, I had never had any interest in religion or spirituality. But now, I had very clear and intense feelings on the subject. I felt no interest in organized religion, but a very strong closeness to God. I had never felt so close to God before in my life. I felt God could whisper in my ear and I could hear the messages. Over time, I would develop my own definite notions of what "God" was, and how it all worked. To this day, I feel I personally understand Jesus, and listen to God, while not subscribing to any formal religion.

Even more than my new sense of spirituality, was a feeling that I was now separate or detached from humans in general. I started seeing "humans" as different from myself. What does that make me? Not human? I do not know. I do not feel I come from an alien planet called Hectar, or CB41, or anything like that. I do not have grey skin, and I am not short or have huge eyes. But part of me does not feel of this world. It is very hard to fully describe this because there are no words for it. I feel "different" and "detached," as if I have one foot in each world. I also feel I have one foot on earth and one foot in the spirit world (in death?). Am I an alien? Well, I was born a human on Earth, so you answer that. I can honestly tell you that I do not shape-shift into a reptile at night. But I can also tell you that I no longer felt "normal."

I realized I could ask the voice in my head questions, and I would sometimes get answers. I could ask, "Do I turn right here or left," and I would get an answer saying, "Left," and the "left" would be the correct answer. There were many examples of this. I also found I could draw upon many different "sources," and not just the one "entity." I found myself very connected to "Source," as they say in psychic circles. "Source," being Universal energy, "God," or "Spirit."

I became a different person. But at the same time, I still had the essence and memories of the old person inside me. I became a new person that consisted of the old and the new, mixed together.

As far as my psychic abilities at the time, I felt I had three major abilities. I could sense what others were feeling and thinking sometimes; I could talk to these voices coming from "Source" (the Universe); and I had a tremendous amount of knowledge available to me that I never had before. There would be much more to come as far as abilities, but those were the major abilities I noticed immediately at the time, if we do not count the fact that I didn't feel totally human anymore.

I spent weeks and months in this dual universe of feeling powerful and smart, but also being completely mentally damaged and non-functional. I felt mentally disabled because I could not cognitively handle more than one task at a time. Just driving to the grocery store had to be planned out step by step. But on the other hand, I had these amazing abilities and abstract thoughts hiding in the back of my head. I knew I was not a genius, but I felt like one in a weird way sometimes.

My new abilities and repressed brainpower were very limited though, because I had a tremendous sadness and depression that lived with me always. I was very subdued. I had not opened my mail in many weeks, and kept a huge pile of unopened mail sitting on the floor in my office.

The truth is that something was very off. Although I was now able to function at minimal levels, my sadness and depression seemed to be escalating. I was really messed up. I had gone through many losses, I had suffered some sort of paranormal mental trauma, I felt like part of me died, I was a totally different person inside with a seemingly totally different personality, and I really could not cope with everything at once. It became so overwhelming for my feeble human mind that I really did not want to live anymore.

The depression was becoming so strong, it was the only feeling I had. But I think what was putting me over the edge was that I was living in this depression in a person that did not feel like me. I felt really lost with the feeling that the "old me" had died. I had no anchor in life, or reference point of existence. All I knew is that my old life was dead, I was totally mired in sadness and depression, and I saw no hope of things changing or getting better. I did not feel insane or controlled by the depression. Deep inside I felt sharper than I had ever felt in my life. But on the outside I was very slow-functioning in some ways. Draped over that contradiction was a depression as black and thick as any molasses you could find.

I found myself for the first time in my life contemplating suicide. I was very thoughtful about it. I did not feel I was being impulsive or insane about it. I was thinking through it, deciding if it was a good option for me, as if it were a business decision. On one hand, I definitely did not want to live anymore, but on the other hand, I felt I had an obligation to live on with whatever this new life was within me.

I thought about suicide for big chunks of the day every day. I knew I probably needed help and a doctor. I needed a doctor for many reasons. Firstly, I wanted to kill myself. But secondly, why did I go from being a very efficient person who could multi-task, to a mentally damaged person who could barely get to the grocery store. I once said to myself, "so this is what it feels like to be stupid." I always had top grades at the top of my class and knew all the business answers and so on. And now I had to think through how I was going to find my car, drive to the store, and then find my car again to come back home and so on. But the other side of this contradiction was the fact I had Albert Einstein in the back of my head trying to explain a Universal principle to me, along with many other ideas and visions about the Universe, space, time, and other foreign concepts I had never given much thought to before in my life. Then I would flip back to literally forgetting where I parked my car. Sometimes I would be in the grocery store and for a few moments, not know where in the store I was, or why I was there. I would look at a list of ten items, and a few moments later not remember one of them. But while trying to decide if I needed eggs, and where the eggs would be, I would be thinking about why humans act in weird ways in certain situations. It was like my mind operated in many different dimensions and levels at the same time.

I started to try and think how I would see a doctor. But like everything else, it became too complicated. I did not know which hospital to go to, or where, or if I was covered by insurance, and how I would even find the hospital and get there. I concluded I needed someone to actually do this for me and take me there, but there was nobody there to do this. Thus, I determined I could not see a doctor. I gave up on that and just kept living what I was living.

Over time, I slowly recovered. Sadness was gone and depression was fading. What remained was my newly revised personality and thoughts. In many ways I acted or thought in similar ways as Chaz did. I had a deeper understanding of things he had been trying to explain to me, and why he was explaining them. I understood more of his hidden motives on various issues. It was an odd combination of me "becoming" what he was, while also "listening" to the mental messages, while also still being myself with my own thoughts and memories.

I am not here trying to claim I am anything in particular, or that I can do magic tricks, or that I know the secrets of the Universe. I am not trying to prove anything, and I am fine if people think I am crazy or don't believe my story. I know what happened to me, I lived it, and I don't wish it upon anyone. But I try to use my unique perspectives to help other people and give ideas that might contribute in some way. I consider myself a mess. What happened to me destroyed my life. I have risen from the ashes and tried to write books and counsel people in pain. Neither of these things were of ANY interest to me before the event by the way. I do remember Chaz suggesting I might make a great author someday though. He said lots of strange things that seemed bizarre at the time, that turned out to be my present reality. I have no explanation for this.

Again, if you desire to read my entire story for full context, including more details of this event, you can find that in my memoir *The Walk-In*. I am sorry if this sounds like a tease, but I literally cannot include that entire book into this one, and at the same time it is only fair I disclose that my full accounting including the lead-up and after effects, are available if you want to inspect my accounting in deeper detail. But it's not for everyone, and especially not for the squeamish. Enough on that.

I do not have all the answers, but I do have my accounting of what happened to me. Perhaps by sharing my experiences, they can be used someday by others in finding provable answers to some questions. For our purposes in this book, I feel this incident is very important, and might give us clues as to how aliens perhaps interact with humans on a consciousness level through walk-ins or otherwise. I'm not saying Chaz was an alien of some sort, but maybe I am saying that.

CHAPTER THREE

What And Who
Are Aliens?

I was not a fan of writing the first two chapters about my own experiences. I don't want this book to be about me. But I wrote about my experiences for a couple of reasons. First, I believe a major purpose of this book is to work toward removing the stigmas associated with experiencing, and sharing your experiences, of paranormal and supernatural events. We also need to destigmatize the word "alien" to not automatically mean that anyone who says the word is crazy. Additionally, I purposely wanted to share those two very different experiences as a way of setting the stage for our discussions on what aliens are, what encounters we might have, and how we should think of aliens going forward.

This is the point in the book where I might do the very cliched thing of talking about each and all of the various alien species that are out there. However, I am not going to do that, and sorry if that disappoints you. There are several reasons for not doing this. First of all, I do not know all of the various alien species out there. To identify and describe all of the alien species out there would be far more difficult than trying to list and describe all species of life on earth, whether it be animal, bird, insect, or so on. Even on Earth, we are still learning about new species of life all the time. So imagine trying to tackle species of life in the Universe. I believe there are other books out there that attempt to provide information on many different alien species. I don't know where they get their information, and I will leave that task to them.

However crazy and outlandish many of my assertions of knowledge are going to be in this book, I am only providing theories and information on topics and subjects with which I feel I have some direct or indirect knowledge or experience. I am not going to repost information from other sources, nor am I going to simply make up random information to fill a book. I am going to stick to the core group of items and subjects to which I feel I can constructively contribute. People can still be skeptical and cynical of me or things I say, but at least I can personally feel that I am able to stand behind my own opinions and beliefs without looking left or right at other sources telling me what I should be thinking or saying.

I am completely fine with you being skeptical, cynical, or disagreeing with things I say in this book. I fully expect that. My goal is never to tell anyone what to think, or try to convince anyone of my positions. My goal always is to open minds, encourage people to think for themselves, and to contribute my own experiences and knowledge to the growing base of evidence in this field of research and philosophy. Until some of us are able to provide absolute concrete proof of what we feel we know to be true, nobody is totally right, and nobody is totally wrong. We should all listen to the experiences out there and decide for ourselves how we feel about them.

With that said, let's clear up a definition issue. I am using the word "alien" in this book. Many will say I should be using the word "extraterrestrial." They are kind of right, but they aren't actually. They are correct in the sense that "alien" is kind of a slang term for extraterrestrial. It makes me sound unprofessional, unsophisticated, and kind of a hack to be using the term "alien." But I am using the term alien for specific reasons. First of all, I don't care what people think of me. But more importantly, using the term "extraterrestrial" would be inaccurate in my context. Why is that, you ask? Well, an extraterrestrial refers to a being that is not from planet Earth. In the context which I will be explaining, I believe aliens are already on Earth, and therefore I will be discussing aliens that are from Earth, in addition to those that are not. By using the word alien, I am simply talking about intelligent beings that are not completely human. I could just as well use the term "nonhumans," but aliens sounds more fun and intriguing, doesn't it? So, aliens it is.

As I previously mentioned, I am interested in adding to the conversation about aliens, and not just repeating established conversations. Therefore, I have decided not to fully focus on commonly known species of aliens such as "The Greys" and "Reptilians." Also, I am not happy with the narrow focus regarding alien species. I think it is a mistake for humans to think too narrowly about what an alien might be. When you say the word "alien" to most people, they usually think of "The Greys." They think of those little grey (or green) men with short bodies, big heads, and big eyes. I think it is a mistake to reinforce this image of aliens.

I believe the chances are good that the first alien you ever come into contact with in your life won't be a little grey or green man with a big head and big eyes. I believe the first alien you may have already come into contact with, would have looked human. This is not my guarantee, but I will explain to you why I feel this way. I also wish to stress that we may encounter other types of aliens which we have not ever imagined possible. Humans need to be conditioned to keep a very open mind as to what they might see when they do come across aliens. One thing I guarantee is that nothing is as it seems, and nothing is the way you think it is or perhaps wish it to be. Therefore, whatever you think of in terms of aliens is not the reality. My best advice is to expect the unexpected and think outside the box. This means keeping an open mind. This means I will be spending much of the book trying to break stereotypes and expectations.

With all that said, I am not saying "The Greys" or the "Reptilians" do not exist. I believe they do. But I have decided to focus my

43

attention on the aliens that appear more human, or seem completely human. This brings me to a point I was trying to make at the beginning of this chapter. I was explaining why I felt it was important for me to share two of my personal experiences with you. The first experience was a potential abduction, during which I don't remember seeing actual aliens. But the second experience was that of a "walk-in."

Some people may have wondered why I was sharing a walk-in experience in this book. Isn't a walk-in more of a supernatural paranormal event? What does a walk-in have to do with aliens, and thus what is it doing in this book? Well, I specifically put it in this book because I think walk-ins have everything to do with aliens.

If you read the chapter on the walk-in carefully, you will have noticed that the walk-in "suspect" is highly SUSPECT as far as what kind of person, or being, he actually was. After years of thoughts, I have come to the conclusion that one type of alien is an "alien of consciousness." The best way for me to define an "alien of consciousness" is to perhaps say that this is an alien soul, or a soul of an alien. If you don't like the word "soul" for religious or spiritual reasons, let us instead simply use the word "consciousness." The "Alien Consciousness" would be an alien that lives inside a human body or host body. I do not think of this as some kind of "demonic possession," but rather a real legitimate conscious "creature" that lives inside a host body. I hate to joke about this because to me it is personal, but haven't some of you guys seen the old Star Trek episodes where alien entities would take over Captain Kirk or one of the other crew members? Without making a mockery of this subject, that is kind of what I am talking about.

I am suggesting a separate entity or being of consciousness that is made of energy. It can live outside a body, but would have no use of arms, legs, mouth, tongue, or eyes, without a body. Thus, this consciousness lives inside a host body, such as a human, so that it can function as a human, and contribute and express itself in all ways that

44

humans can. Humans are excellent "hosts" because they have plenty of limbs for movement and dexterity, and can experience all senses, emotions, and sensations. Human bodies can also grow and regenerate if damaged. The human body is actually quite an amazing organism if I do say so myself. But I digress.

So what I am doing here is making a suggestion or assertion that a very common species of alien is a "consciousness" that does not actually have a body. Thus, this type of alien will appear to you as human while it is inside its human host. Now you see why I am trying to encourage you not to assume all aliens are tiny little men with big heads and big eyes. Your assumptions and perceptions will deceive you.

In addition to aliens of consciousness, I also want to suggest "genetic aliens." What I mean by genetic aliens, are those HUMANS who may somehow be part alien genetically. These might be humans who were a part of alien genetic engineering or experiments. We will discuss a bit later in the book about "the alien agenda." Included in that discussion will be the theory that aliens have already done plenty of DNA and genetic experiments on humans. This is the reason for all the abductions where humans undergo some sort of testing or sampling, and then are returned safely back to where they were found.

There may indeed be "normal" humans in our society with some of this alien influence within their DNA or genetics. We take them to be totally human and normal, and they may behave totally human and normal. But technically, there may be an alien element to them, and may be connected to aliens in some way they don't even realize. Therefore, they may technically be aliens.

But at the risk of relaxing you too much and making you think that aliens are simply weird humans, I should now swing our considerations back to the likelihood that plenty of aliens are also scary weird looking creatures that our deepest imaginations can, or perhaps can't, even imagine. Most certainly, the majority of aliens in the Universe are

45

creatures very different from humans. We must keep our minds very wide open as to the possibilities. It could be anything from little grey or green men with big eyes, to Reptilian looking creatures, to three-eyed little or big monsters, to blobs that don't look like anything alive, to maybe rocks that shouldn't be alive but are. The Universe is a very large place and I am sure there is a very large range of creatures out there.

With that said, we can focus more on the type of aliens we think humans might be most likely to encounter. This entails trusting some of the personal abduction and close encounter stories that are out there. This should include my theories that aliens are more than just a body. Aliens are also a consciousness that can present themselves as human.

It makes total logical sense that aliens would take a human form. Think about it. If aliens wanted to figure out a way to interact with humans without frightening them or causing a traumatic dangerous reaction, then aliens would naturally figure out that if they could take a human form, that would be the best way forward. Whether an alien takes a human form through consciousness or through genetic engineering, this is a way for aliens to enter the human society in a non-traumatic subtle way.

If aliens are as smart as we assume them to be, we can only conclude and assume that aliens will for certain, infiltrate our society in human form. It is truly the only way aliens would be able to interact freely with humans. So, I'm voting for the idea that this is exactly what has already been done.

This is why I believe you will, or may have already have, come into contact with an alien. You just didn't realize it. This is also why I think nothing is what it seems and nothing seems as it really is. Welcome to the new world. Or should I say, welcome to the Universe.

CHAPTER FOUR

We Are All Aliens

I can see many of you shaking your heads thinking, "Uhh NO, I am not an alien, speak for yourself." Okay. I suppose in society some aliens will identify as human, and some humans will identify as aliens, right? You can be whatever you want to be. But hear me out. I want to have a discussion around the concept that all of us are aliens because all of us either have alien ancestry, or we are alien because our souls, or the essence of our consciousness, comes from the heaven and stars above, rather than here on terrestrial Earth.

Obviously, this chapter is an extension of the previous chapter. We previously discussed how aliens might have a human appearance because there is an alien consciousness element to some humans, or there is a genetic element to some humans that is alien. In this chapter, I want to explore a couple more concepts in addition to the above. I want to discuss the idea of "alien ancestry," and the purely alien nature of human souls.

First up is the idea of alien ancestry. Believe it or not, I am a person of science for the most part. I know that might shock some of you who are starting to think that I am a koo koo bird who believes in aliens, spaceships, and psychic powers. Yes, I believe in all of the things I just mentioned. But I am not a koo koo bird. A koo koo bird is actually slang for a Cuckoo bird, which is famous for its "koo-koo" sound it makes, which is the inspiration for Cuckoo clocks, one of which my mother had when I was a child, and it became so highly annoying that we had to disable it or risk going insane. Perhaps we did not disable it quickly enough for me?

Anyway, where were we? Oh yeah, alien ancestry. Person of science. Despite being a believer in the paranormal and supernatural,

I am also a believer in science. I do believe in evolution. However, I also believe that humans have not yet discovered all of the science out there to be discovered supporting the details of human evolution. Meaning, the science involving evolution still has some missing gaps to fill in, and some other facts to confirm and expand upon. Naturally, humans try to force science to tie up loose ends so that we can make reasonable conclusions of facts. But sometimes when we are tying up loose ends, we are not doing it with absolute scientific fact or proof.

I guess what I am saying is that although I am a believer in science and evolution, I am not convinced that all humans evolved from something that crawled out of water onto land, and then became part of the ape family, and then became the humans we know of today. Besides, plenty of very legitimate scientists who are one hundred times more educated and smarter than I am, actually disagree with each other on all of the aspects and steps of evolution. So there is that. Basically, we are not sure.

Obviously, evolution has played a major part in human development. I think most people can at least agree on that. I also fully realize there are many people of religious beliefs who believe that humans came about in a very different way other than evolution. So perhaps in the end, none of us agree on anything at all anyways.

But for the purposes of this particular discussion in this chapter, I would like to lay the premise that while evolution has played a huge role in human development, I also believe there may have been some alien ancestry involved. What do I mean by "alien ancestry?" With this term, I am referring to the idea that the humans of today are descendants of prior ancient civilizations that were not of this Earth.

If we are to start from present day and go backwards in time, we would have to consider that there were past civilizations on Earth that we know little or nothing about. How did the pyramids get built? Did humans as we know them today really manage to lift those huge stones way up to the top without any modern machinery and equipment? Why are there so many ancient structures that are built perfectly in alignment with the stars, sun cycles, and astronomical principles without any modern knowledge or devices? Why are their ancient carvings that depict creatures that appear to be alien in nature? Questions, question, so many questions.

Clearly there is more to be discovered about our human ancient ancestors, who we cannot actually prove were totally human. That is the point now, isn't it? We can't prove they were not of some alien origin. We have discovered skulls that we also can't fully explain as to whether they are more human in nature, or more ape in nature, or something in between, or none of the above. Scientists struggle to stuff square pegs into round holes so that we can maintain our basic theories of how we think things evolved. But if we are to be truthful, square pegs don't really fit into round holes. The truth is that science still has much more to discover before it can provide a complete and confirmed picture of evolution, and how things started as far as humanity goes.

With all of that said above, let us assume we can somehow justify or prove that those ancient ancestors were indeed fully human. Where did THEY come from originally? I have a question to answer the question. Where did the Earth come from? The Earth came from the Universe. If you believe the Big Bang Theory, the Earth was formed through a huge explosion from a singularity, black hole, or what have you. I love the phrase "what have you," don't you? Yes, we don't know for sure is what that means. But can we at least agree that the Earth came from the Universe? The Earth did not come from the Earth. That much we can agree, I hope. So, if the Earth came from the Universe, then life on Earth would have come from the Universe. That means that life on Earth would have come from some other place than Earth. Well, if life on Earth came from some place other than Earth, than that means it was alien. This means life on

Earth was alien in nature. It then became known as being native to Earth and lost its "alien status." But originally, the seed of life for Earth would have been alien in nature. This means all life on Earth started out as alien.

The other possibility is that after the Earth was formed, aliens from other planets colonized Earth. It is also possible that some of what I said above is truth, and other parts are not. Or it could be true that everything we know of, is all true at the same time. For example, perhaps aliens colonized Earth, but those civilizations died off, leaving primitive ape-like humans to claim Earth, who then evolved into the humans we know today.

I don't want to get ahead of myself. I do not want to claim I know everything or even much of anything about evolution, science, archaeology, or anthropology. I don't. I am only suggesting logical possibilities to open our minds for discussion. Many things are possible until certain things are proven to be true or proven to be not true.

I tend to believe that many contradicting facts can still co-exist together in ways humans have not fully understood yet. What I am suggesting is that I believe both alien ancestry theory and classical human evolution theory could both be true together at the same time. Humans like to think in binary terms where it is one or the other. However, most of life is not binary. Most of life is multidimensional and complex in nature. I actually discuss these topics in my book *EVOLVE*. I don't want to beat this subject to death, but I felt it was very important to consider it in our discussions because I believe we probably do have alien ancestry in our lineage. That would make us aliens.

Now let us consider the other concept I was suggesting regarding our souls. IF you believe that humans have souls, and that is a big IF for some people, then you must realize those souls are a collection of intelligent energy that comes from the Universe above. I know people

50

have different religious and spiritual beliefs about the human soul. I don't disrespect anyone's beliefs. You should keep your beliefs as you like them. But for those who believe in this concept of the human soul being a separate entity from the body, you might then consider that the soul came from a different place other than Earth.

Whether a soul came from God, Heaven, the Universe, or some other place, the soul did not come from Earth. If that is the case, then the soul would be considered extraterrestrial and alien. This discussion of souls then relates to my previous concept of "aliens of consciousness." Perhaps souls are independent beings that sometimes exist separate from bodies, and sometimes exist within bodies. When souls are not within a body, are they floating freely in the Universe? Does this mean they are aliens?

Have you noticed how so many "souls" of people, are different? Have you noticed how different everyone is from each other? It is almost as if everyone is alien from each other. Meaning, everyone is alien from each other because they are so different. A play on words perhaps. I know many people feel like they are aliens, because they feel they don't fit into society. Most of us at some point in our lives have felt like aliens. We have not felt included, or that we didn't fit into society.

Notice now I am speaking about all of us in the most human sense. Even in the most human sense, we are in many ways aliens. Even as humans, we are alone within ourselves, feeling very different from all people and everything that surround us. We wonder why we are here. Why were we left here on this planet, in this society, only to feel so alone? It literally is as if we feel like aliens within our own species, on our own planet, in our own society.

Well, I suggest that this feeling might be your inner-most soul whispering to you that you feel this way because maybe some way, somehow, is indeed alien. Or you are an alien. In a way, we are all aliens as the chapter title suggests.

The final question would be, does it matter? We put such importance on labeling. We label people based upon different types, genders, races, colors, sizes, appearance, and now species. Should it matter if someone is male or female? Should it matter what color someone is? Does this affect how we treat them? Should it matter? Then why should it matter what species someone is? Human or alien, does it matter? As we continue on in this book, I hope you continue to consider whether or not it really should matter at all what someone is. Beings do not get to choose what they are. What matters more is WHO someone is, and that is something each individual gets to define for themselves. What someone chooses is much more important than what they were not allowed to choose. You must accept what you couldn't choose, but you must choose wisely where you are given choice to do so. We should love and support those trying to make the right choices, regardless of what they are. This goes for humans and aliens both.

CHAPTER FIVE

Are Aliens Good Or Bad?

What do you think? Are aliens good or bad? We all want to know, right? I think it is safe to say that almost all humans FEAR aliens, but that does not necessarily mean that aliens are "bad," does it? I think before we answer that question we need to define what we mean by "bad."

Let's think about a lion. Is a lion bad? Most people would say that lions are beautiful animals. They are wonderful and deserve to be protected. Does this mean lions are "good?" Well, I think if you ask a six-year-old, they would say lions are good. In many cases I trust a six-year-old more than many adults, so I am inclined to accept their answer that lions are "good."

But what would happen if I asked a zebra if lions are good or bad? What would the zebra's answer be? I suppose a zebra would first flinch at the word "lion," and wonder if there was one lurking and about to attack. A zebra would associate a lion with being a creature that wants to kill and eat it. I doubt a zebra would say a lion is good.

So where does that leave us? We have one vote for "good lion," and one vote for "bad lion." The moral of the story is that whether something is good or bad will often depend on who you ask. The same is going to apply to whether or not aliens are good or bad, and whether they are good or bad for humans. I will explain more in a minute.

But first, let's examine our opinion of the aliens we feel are currently observing Earth and abducting humans. If these aliens were "bad," then they likely would have already wiped us out. Certainly, these aliens have the technology to do away with humans if they wanted. But they haven't. Instead, these aliens seem to be quite gentle in remaining mostly invisible, and when they take invasive actions, such as abductions, they return the humans intact and unharmed, from their perspective.

Therefore, I submit to you that the aliens humans are likely currently dealing with are "good." Again, your opinion and perspective of what good and bad means will cause you to have your own opinions. My own standard is that anything that does not kill me or eat me might be good. Yes, I have set the bar pretty low. Humanity has caused me to set the bar low. Call it human conditioning from living here within human society. Regardless, please humor me for a minute and let's run with the assumption that the current aliens are "good."

Now let's muddy the waters and thicken the plot by considering the fact that the Universe is a big place, and within the Universe there is darkness and light. There is good and bad. Even if you don't want to believe that there is evil out there, allow us to consider the animal kingdom here on Earth.

I want to look at the animal kingdom on Earth because I think it represents an example of how even when there is no good or bad, there is still a pyramid of threats, which can be perceived as bad depending on who or what you are. For example, let's go back to the lion and the zebra. Without playing clever mind games, we can all pretty much agree that both lions and zebras are good, since they are both beautiful animals of Earth. However, the zebras most definitely view the lions as bad. So from a zebra's point of view, lions are definitely bad, even though lions are not bad from our perspective. Thus, even when there is no good and bad, there is still good and bad from the perspective of certain beings.

I say all of this to illustrate the point that regardless of whether or not you think there is good and evil out in the Universe, we should all agree that there is definitely likely to be some bad things out there from the perspective of humans. Think of humans as zebras. There are likely some "lions" out there in the Universe that are a threat to humans, and thus humans would consider them as bad.

Therefore, let us assume there are "lions" out there in the Universe that humans ("zebras") would consider bad for them. Next, let us remind ourselves of how infinitely huge the Universe is. The only conclusion to be reached is that there are most certainly some "bad aliens" out there in the Universe somewhere.

Thus, the answer to the question of whether aliens are good or bad is both, "yes they are good," and, "yes they are bad." In other words, some aliens are good and some aliens are bad. Let us take solace in the idea that the aliens currently surrounding us are good. But let us not forget there are also bad aliens out there somewhere that perhaps have not discovered us yet. The emphasis should be on YET.

What should humans do about this? This is a lot to take in at once. First, we have to get comfortable with the idea that the "scary" aliens (scary to humans) currently interacting with us are probably good. Most humans will need some time just to chew on that for a while. However, the more difficult item to digest is the fact that there ARE bad aliens out there somewhere, and what does that mean for humans.

While the current aliens seem good, I think the good news about bad aliens is that the bad ones have not encountered us yet. I say this because we are still here. If bad aliens had found us, we would know it by now, because we would likely be either gone, or obviously victimized in some way. So far the only victimizing I see happening here on Earth is humans victimizing other humans.

So where are these bad aliens? When will they find us? What will happen when they find us? All good questions. You need to again think of the Universe as a huge place. Let's scale it down so it is easier to visualize. Pretend for a minute that the entire Earth is equivalent to the entire Universe. Let's say an ant represents humans. Let's say a lizard represents the bad aliens. Of course, I could have said REPTILIAN lizard to represent bad aliens, but that would be considered racist against Reptilian aliens, so I won't do that. We should not use stereotypes against any species, or race to demonize them.

We have an ant as humans, and a lizard as bad aliens. Let's say the ant is located in The Bahamas and the lizard is located in Australia. What are the chances of that lizard finding the ant? Not very good. The lizard would have to find a way to traverse the huge expanse of oceans and somehow get lucky enough to land on the Bahamas Islands. But even if the lizard made it to The Bahamas by some unlikely miracle, the lizard would still have to somehow find the ant. That would still be almost impossible really. What I am saying is that there is a good chance that bad aliens will never find Earth.

They will never find Earth unless they already have. What I mean by that is that it is possible that in Earth's ancient history, bad aliens did indeed find Earth, and wiped out human civilizations, or beings that came before humans. Here on Earth we have some unsettled ancient history questions about what happened to previous civilizations. We have evidence of great pyramids, buried cities, and cities underwater. We have no proof of how these ancient civilizations got there, or who built them.

How could it be possible that entire hugely developed civilizations lived here on Earth, and we have no record of who they were? It is as if they just vanished. That makes no sense. How could entire civilizations just vanish? The answer would have to involve some major cataclysmic event that is either climate related, supernatural, or outer-worldly. Perhaps there was an alien attack that exterminated civilizations on Earth?

This is why it is very important that ancient alien historians,

56

archaeologists, scientists, and researchers of all stripes continue their work to try and discover some answers to these important questions. If it can be determined that Earth was indeed attacked in ancient history by some other worldly or alien species, then we need to know this so we can contemplate possible future threats.

However, regardless of whether or not Earth had already encountered and been attacked by bad aliens or not, we still have the reality of knowing that bad aliens must exist out there in the Universe somewhere.

These bad aliens might be evil like some evil humans, or these bad aliens might just be predators like the lion. Both are bad for humans. Whether humans are wiped out from evil aliens who love killing, or whether humans are wiped out from aliens who are just hunting like lions, the result is the same for humans, and not good.

What should humans do about the prospect of someday being unlucky enough to encounter bad aliens? Should we get out our hunting rifles and sling shots, and fight to the death? Will that be effective? Should we set off all our nuclear warheads in an effort to defeat the bad aliens? Would blowing the Earth and ourselves up actually defeat the bad aliens successfully anyway? Or would it just mean we blew ourselves and the planet up because we are that stupid?

Do we think we can battle an alien species that is thousands of years ahead of us technologically? Humans who don't even like each other and have very limited technologies, are going to compete against an alien species that has the ability to travel lightyears through space? I don't know about you, but I am not liking the odds of success in this scenario. I have a feeling that shooting a missile at an alien starship will only result in pissing them off, and not result in any damage to them. In fact, I am very confident that all useful weapons would be easily disabled by the aliens before they could even be used by us.

Don't get too depressed by all this talk. I am not here just to be a downer and ruin any party I go to. I have an idea. All is not lost. Cheer up, we still have a chance. I think I have an idea. Let me know what you think.

What if we created an alliance with the good aliens who have already been observing us for so long? The good aliens have the advanced technology to compete with the bad aliens. Perhaps we can look to them for protection? A similar analogy would be how third world developing countries here on Earth seek protection from military super powers if they can arrange it. The super-power countries will often provide that defense because they may have interests in the region. How is this situation I have outlined with good aliens different? Perhaps the good aliens have interests in this region of the galaxy, and with Earth or humans specifically, and therefore would find it advantageous to provide assistance and defend Earth and humans against the bad aliens.

How are you starting to feel about the good aliens now? It might be that they are crucial for the safety and survival of human civilizations on Earth. Perhaps humans have been thinking of them in the wrong way. Instead of being terrified and aggressive toward them, maybe we should be encouraging contact with them. It might actually be in our best interests to build and develop a strong relationship with the aliens as soon as possible.

Could it be this concept of the aliens providing a defense for Earth is the reason they have been here all along? It could be part of their agenda, or reason for being around Earth in this part of the galaxy. Perhaps our alien friends are already aware of possible threats to us in this part of the Universe, and they are here to maintain security and safety for this part of the galaxy.

We have to open our minds and think more clearly and logically. It is not lost upon me that the previous statement might seem totally hilarious considering that I have just been ranting about aliens attacking and defending Earth. How can clear and logical thinking be in the same room as rantings about aliens? Perhaps from a skeptical frightened human perspective it cannot. But from a different perspective, what I have said is very clear, logical, and possible. I am not writing this book to convince anyone of anything. I am simply opening minds up to the possibilities surrounding us. It's a huge buffet I offer you, and you may eat only what you want, if anything.

We started this chapter by wondering if the aliens we believe are zipping around Earth are good or bad. I hope I succeeded in expanding the discussion, as well as ideas, perspectives, and possibilities. Good or bad in the case of humans will be judged upon our ability to survive and prosper. If aliens can help us survive and prosper, then that is a good thing in my view. Fear has always been one of humanity's biggest weaknesses. Let us not allow fear to doom us from opportunities here, and out there. Our future may depend on it.

CHAPTER SIX

The Alien Agenda

So what do they want, anyways? Why are they coming here? Why are they already here? Why are they abducting humans? All good questions. Let us explore the answers.

It is very important to think like an alien when considering the answers to the above questions. If you think like a human, you will be led astray. Humans usually think from a place of fear and aggression. That is their nature. So naturally, humans often think aliens must be coming to take over Earth, or for some other dubious reason. This human type of thinking is ridiculous right out of the box. Why? Well, let us employ some logic and sound reasoning. What we know for sure is that aliens have technology far more advanced than what humans have. Therefore, if aliens wanted to "take over Earth," they could do so at any time with very little effort. They would have done so hundreds or thousands of years ago already. So, you can put away your hunting rifle, sling shot, and baseball bat. You won't need them to fight off aliens. And any of you feeling super tough and thinking we can just use nuclear weapons against them, well think again. Aliens would have the technology to disable the arming of them, and even if humans succeeded in using them, they are only blowing themselves up, along with their own planet up in the progress.

Therefore, do you think we can take "Earth invasion" off the table? I think so. What about aliens trying to gain access to human intelligence and technology? Yeah, you can laugh, because I know I am. So that's a "no" also. Why are aliens interested in us then? If humans are inferior to aliens mentally and technologically, and they seem to not want to take over Earth since they have the ability to do so but have never done so, then what can it be?

Before I answer that, I want to make it clear that aliens have multiple agendas where humans and Earth are concerned. One of the obvious is to maintain some security within this sector of the galaxy. There are other reasons also, but for this book I want to focus on the single most important and intriguing answer of them all. The answer lies within the question of what makes humans UNIQUE. Logically speaking, aliens would only have interest in humans if there is something interesting about humans. Or, aliens would be interested in humans if humans have something that aliens don't have but want. And if humans have something that aliens do not have, then why don't aliens just take it?

The answer is that humans have something that aliens do not have, but that aliens can't simply "take." Humans have something very interesting to aliens. Or perhaps I should say that humans are unique in a very special way that is different from aliens.

How many pages can I go on teasing about this answer? Surely, I can drag this out for much longer without actually giving an answer, can't I? Okay, well, since you are likely already annoyed with me already, I better stop now. The answer is that aliens are quite interested in what makes humans unique from other species of the Universe, including them. The thing that makes humans very unique from other species is their strong and intense ability to sense emotions and sensations.

Humans are possibly one of the most EMOTIONAL "beings of intelligence" in the Universe. Humans are somehow capable of developing scientific technologies, while at the same time thinking and acting with emotion most of the time. This is indeed very unique and interesting. You would think that a species who does not think with logic, but rather with emotion, would be incapable of much productive technology. Yet, humans have been capable of significant

61

technological progress over short periods of time, while still exhibiting totally irrational, out of control, and even crazy behaviors.

Think about people you know who are amazing at their jobs. They might go to work and be brilliant at what they do. But when they go home, they may have a half dozen vices they are a victim to, or have horrible, failed relationships, or basically collapse into a corner emotionally broken. We have all known, or at least witnessed, people like this. This is fascinating to aliens. Train wrecks of people who can still do brilliant things. What a paradox! There is no consistency in behavior or thought with humans. One minute they appear as bumbling, broken, and emotionally irrational beings, but the next minute they are capable of very focused intelligent thought. When humans are emotional, they are somewhat useless, but when they are focused and logical, they are quite productive. A paradox is always interesting, regardless of what Universe species you may be.

However, what I have described so far is not even the true interest and motivation for the aliens' interest in humans. The true interest in humans is the humans' ability to FEEL extremely strong emotions and sensations. Humans are capable of feeling love, sadness, happiness, anger, and passion at levels that are off the charts from an alien's perspective.

You have to remember that an alien culture that is so incredibly successful at technology, structure, planning, organization, and patience, is a culture based upon logic and very disciplined thinking. There is no room for emotional irrationality in an alien culture. Their minds are very logical and disciplined. Thus, aliens are fascinated by emotion and sensations.

What do I mean by "sensations?" Sensations are related and connected to emotions. Sensations are what we feel emotionally when we have physical contact with certain things. An example of this would be the sensation of taste. When humans eat their favorite foods, they have a very intense sensation of taste that is so strong, it directly

62

affects their emotions. A human can actually experience a mental orgasm just by eating certain foods. Now imagine being an alien watching this. Imagine seeing a creature enjoy certain foods so much that their eyes roll back in their heads. Wouldn't you find that intriguing?

And speaking of eyes rolling back in their heads, let's talk about sex. Humans have a sexual experience that surely beats many species out there. Sexual gratification is more intense for some humans than other humans, but most can agree that the human sexual experience is very intense. The human orgasm is so intense that even humans themselves are amazed by it.

Logically, such an intense amazing orgasm is not necessary for procreation. An alien species can logically decide if they want offspring, and can interact with their mate through the breeding process in order to accomplish the creation of offspring. It is a loving business decision, and the act of breeding does not need to offer any kind of extra incentive, such as an orgasm. The desire to create offspring with a mate is plenty incentive enough to engage in the act of breeding.

But not humans! Humans get to have this amazing orgasmic breeding experience that is so great, that humans engage in the act of breeding even when they have no intention or desire to create offspring. How illogical is that? Humans will carry out the act of breeding even though they don't want to breed. Curious creatures these humans!

As an alien watching all of this, you might wonder why humans were so lucky to be gifted with such strong, intense, and amazing emotions and sensations. Surely these emotions and sensations make the experience of living life so much better. Perhaps as an alien you would want to experience more out of your life experience like humans get to do.

Just imagine if you could have the superior intellect and behavior of an alien, but also the amazing gift of emotions and sensations that humans have. That combination would be the ultimate Universal being. Read that previous line again.

Therein you have the motivation for why aliens are interested in humans. The question for aliens is HOW do humans possess this ability for emotions and sensations that are so strong and amazing. Secondly, HOW can aliens introduce these traits into their own species safely and productively?

What would it require to figure this out? Well, a few things. It would require a lot of research into human anatomy, human psychology, human development, and most importantly, human DNA. Based upon the aforementioned, what would you expect aliens to do then? Well, you would expect aliens to have a research program that observes humans for a long period of time, while also taking plenty of DNA samples they can study.

Aliens would approach all of this in a very logical and brilliant way. They would observe from many different perspectives and methods. They would physically observe person to person, or rather alien to human. They would observe by trying to get into the heads of humans, meaning gaining access to the human psyche. They would observe societal behavior. They would observe human evolution through time and history. They would observe human behavior, as well as human technology. The angles of observation would be almost infinite. But that would not be enough.

Aliens would also need actual physical samples from humans. They would need blood samples, DNA samples, and semen/sperm samples. It is also possible they have found a way to harmlessly take brain tissue samples. They would be trying to figure out the anatomical and DNA factors that might account for the human ability of emotion and sensation.

This is where we get to talk about abductions again. Consider all of the stories of abductions. Most of the stories include accounts of being taken, but not harmed. The accounts often include instances of some sort of invasive sample taken. In my case, I had my thumb punctured. I have heard of other cases where semen and sperm samples were taken. You can go through all of the abduction cases you know of, and almost all of them include some kind of testing or taking of samples.

Fortunately, aliens seem to have a motivation of not harming humans in the process of collecting samples. Are there some samples they need which do require harm? Maybe. What comes to mind for me are the incidences of cattle mutilation. There have been unexplained cases of cattle being drained of blood, eyes removed, and most interesting to me, the tongue removed. Are you thinking what I am thinking? For me, the removal of the tongue is an indication of aliens needing a tongue sample so that they can try and figure out the sensation of taste. They obviously don't want to cut the tongue out of a human, but perhaps they feel okay doing it to a cow? This might seem cruel to many, but you have to remember that aliens are logical creatures. It would be very logical for aliens to conclude that it is acceptable to kill and cut the tongue out of a cow BECAUSE that is precisely what humans do to cows. Surely, if it is okay to kill a cow and cut the tongue out in the human culture, then it would be acceptable for aliens to use cows for the same purpose without violating human cultural boundaries.

At any rate, aliens are collecting all of this observational data on humans, as well as actual tissue and DNA samples. All of this is in hopes of figuring out how these humans have such unique and powerful emotions and sensations. Aliens want to keep their intellect, but want to somehow introduce these emotional experiences into their own DNA.

All of this raises the next issue. It would be logical for aliens to consider inter-breeding experiments. What would happen if you bred a human with a particular alien species? Would that breeding exercise

65

result in a "super-human" and "super-alien" that has the advanced intellect of an alien, but also with the human emotions and sensations?

What would be the best way to conduct this type of breeding experiment? Is it best to take sperm samples from humans, and then develop fetuses in test tubes, or even inseminate aliens? Or is the best way to introduce alien DNA into human females? Should they try to impregnate human females on the alien spacecraft? Or should they introduce a hybrid alien human onto Earth, and then have that alien DNA carrier breed normally with a human female?

This all plays into the question of whether aliens, or part aliens (hybrids), are already here. Part of the alien research program would be developing ways to produce alien species that have the appearance of humans. Imagine if your civilization had been doing human DNA work for hundreds or thousands of years. Imagine all of the knowledge and advancements that would have been made during that time. Surely, aliens have mastered the ability to manipulate DNA and create almost any kind of creature they please. It is very likely they have developed the ability to create humans. They would be human in most every way, except not born on Earth and not fully human from a human's perspective. But from a biological and anatomical perspective, they might be totally human. Perhaps from a DNA perspective they are all human, or just partially human. Perhaps they look human, but their behavior and intellect are not very human. Would humans on Earth notice the difference? I doubt it. Humans are not very smart in the sense that humans only consider things that are within their very narrow view of reality. Since humans would never even consider that another person was from an alien breeding program, they would never get suspicious of an alien human or hybrid, even if that alien human acted very differently, or had advanced abilities that most Earth humans do not have.

Regardless of the full extent or methods used, we have to accept the probability that there are breeding experiments happening between humans and aliens. Yes, the humans participating might not fully realize this. But certainly aliens are trying to determine the optimal "DNA recipe" for creating a species of human aliens or alien humans that have the best traits from both species.

You can decide for yourself if you feel this is ethical, good, bad, constructive, or otherwise. But I feel this gives us an insight into the alien psyche. Clearly, the aliens feel this is ethical and productive. They feel they can abduct humans, take samples, and then conduct breeding experiments. I say it like it's a bad thing. It sounds harsh. However, it is also obvious that aliens go through a lot of effort to try and make the abduction process as fast as possible while not harming the human. This is proof that there IS a certain ethic involved with their methods. They are clearly not a brutal ruthless species. They are far more gentle than humans would be in a similar circumstance. So before you start throwing stones at the alien agenda, you might want to consider how humans act toward other species, and how humans have acted toward other races of humans during times of medical research, and certainly during conflict. Some might even say that humans have no moral ground to judge other species who are peacefully conducting research in a harmless way.

With that said, most humans and abductees can agree that we did not consent to being sampled and having samples taken from us. Certainly, it is very intrusive for males to have sperm samples forcibly taken from them. I am not sure aliens fully understand the human psyche when it comes to human sexuality. Sperm samples being taken from human males without consent would constitute rape from a moral perspective. It is a highly personal thing. But this is exactly the point, isn't it? The fact that aliens don't fully understand the EMOTIONS behind such things. This is why aliens are studying humans. They WANT to understand why humans are so emotional about certain things.

For example, if humans love having sex and love having an orgasm so much, then why would a male feel violated by being stimulated into giving a sperm sample? To an alien this is a paradox. To a human it is obvious why this is offensive. I have been interested over the years to see or hear about different accounts of abductions. Some include males being brought to orgasm sexually, while others are accounts of samples being taken by needle. Honestly, I don't prefer the latter. But if the accounts are true and honest, it shows a desire by the aliens to try and gain their samples in the most effective and least offensive way possible. They likely have not figured out the best way, since most humans would disagree on which way, or any way, would be more acceptable.

I think the overall point I am trying to make is that despite how you feel about intrusive abductions, I believe the intent of the aliens is to do their research and get their samples in the least harmful and least offensive way to humans that they possibly can. This intent shows a benevolent nature.

If you are still offended, then I think you should consider how humans have programs where they capture birds and fish, to then clip fins or wings, and install tracking devices on them. Is it fair for humans to forcibly capture another being and "clip them," "tag them," and "track them?" Well, humans do it for benevolent reasons, right? Humans are trying to learn about the species, and in the end are trying to HELP the species, yes? How is what the aliens are doing to humans different than what humans do to other species in research?

At least aliens are not keeping humans in cages and infecting them with disease on purpose, like humans are doing to monkeys. Humans are arrogance creatures. Humans think they can do unto others, but others should never do unto them. Sorry, but that is unfair and illogical.

So again, what is the alien agenda? I believe it is very similar to the human agenda. I believe it is a benevolent research study to improve and advance their own existence, while also possibly helping the species they are studying. I feel I am being very generous in that statement regarding humans. But with respect to aliens, they have shown nothing but restraint, patience, and consideration in their research regarding humans.

Aliens have the power, technology, and ability to forcibly wipe out humans, and take whatever they want by force. However, they don't do that. Why? Humans probably would. Clearly, aliens have a much higher level of morality than humans perhaps? Maybe this fact is part of the experiment. Maybe aliens seek to give themselves the gift of emotions and sensation, and in exchange will give humans the gift of a higher intellect and morality. Is that a fair trade? Why would humans be against this?

Perhaps this exchange has, or is, already taking place. Maybe we will continue to see an increase in the number of humans showing advanced abilities with a higher than normal level of empathy and morality. Maybe we will see a change in humans while we also see a change in aliens. Perhaps we have already seen aliens who have a human appearance with the emotions and sensations, but the alien intellect still intact. Perhaps we are seeing two species merging into one.

CHAPTER SEVEN

The Government And Aliens

W hat does the government know about aliens? What is the government not telling us? These are questions many have been asking since the Roswell incident. Before we start our discussion, we need to define what "the government" is. For our discussions, "the government" refers to the official governments and militaries of any country that have the technology to track, detect, and study the issue of UFOs and aliens. So, we are primarily talking about the USA government, but also the UK, Russian, Chinese, and all others with a significant military and resources to fully engage in the concern of UFOs and aliens.

I want to start with the premise that aliens are engaged in all areas of Earth. There will be UFO and alien activity in the poorest and most remote areas of Africa, just as likely as in the popular UFO hot spots of the USA. The difference though, is that alien engagement in remote parts of Africa will not be as detected and documented as engagements within the USA. Furthermore, governments and military within remote parts of Africa are not as equipped to detect and track alien activity, and therefore cannot have the level of concern and engagement as other places that do have the ability to detect and track all air traffic and anomalies.

I am saying all of this because I think it is ridiculous to think that alien contact only happens in "famous" places. The USA in some ways has kind of taken ownership of the UFO phenomenon. That is only because the USA has the greatest ability to detect and document such occurrences. I am sure if you visited remote tribes in Africa and Brazil, they would have stories to tell of strange things they have seen at night.

Now that I have laid out that preface and disclosure, we will be referring mostly to the USA government in this discussion, but it can apply to your own government as well if you are not in the USA. Many governments with a substantial military have files on UFO and alien encounters and related phenomena.

So, how much does the government know about aliens? Does it know anything at all? What is the government keeping secret, and why? First, let us lay out the premise that the government knows plenty about aliens. I can say this because we know the US military has extremely sophisticated and powerful systems, equipment, technology, and intelligence, all in a very vast geographic network that is capable of detecting any and all aircraft activity. Furthermore, the US government has a vast network of space satellites capable of doing the same. It is safe to say that the military in this day and age can detect any aircraft within its airspace, and far beyond. Obviously, there is also technology to identify almost all of the aircraft it detects, whether they be commercial airliners or military aircraft.

If we marry the idea that there is alien spacecraft out there, along with the idea that the US military can detect all aircraft, you easily come to the assumption that the US military and US government have knowledge of alien aircraft engagement within the USA, and likely most of Earth.

The US government has admitted publicly, and released video of, UFO encounters. But is this all the government knows? Have they released all the evidence of UFOs and aliens that they are aware of? Of course not. A government, or even business, or even private citizens for that matter, never show their poker hand. Right? All of us might tell a small part of the truth, but we keep almost all of our knowledge about something to ourselves. We want to keep a competitive edge over others by not telling everything we know. We tell just enough to satisfy others that we answered the question. Or, we tell just enough to hopefully initiate a discussion that might result in others revealing things that they know, which we did not know. It's all a game.

My view is that the US government released a "taste" of what they have documented in order to convince people they are being transparent, and to hopefully initiate conversations that might result in some new leads for them in their own research programs.

With that said, I believe the US government is lightyears ahead of where we think they are. I believe they have full knowledge of aliens and alien spacecraft. They may have even had first-hand encounters. Their vast military technology and resources almost makes it impossible for them to not know quite a bit about what it going on regarding alien activity around Earth.

What is the government hoping to accomplish with its alien engagement programs? I believe there are two primary goals. First, and most obviously, they are trying to gain access to alien technology. The first government to have access to alien technology will have a huge advantage over all others on Earth. But secondly, I think the US government wants to be the ones to have the closest alliance with aliens. If the aliens are the ultimate super power, then certainly you would want to become their best friends.

This is where I think there is a divide in our military and government. I believe there are forces within our government and military that view aliens as a threat, and want to take an aggressive posture against them. Then there are others who view aliens as more of a "nature type" or technological research project, and want to approach them in a very friendly benevolent way. You have likely read enough of this book to see which group I am more in alignment with.

The motivation for the US government is clear and strong. Having access to alien technology, and having perhaps an exclusive alliance with the aliens, is such an overwhelming incredible and important incentive, that with certainty it warrants the government's attention and a huge amount of resources in pursuing those goals.

That is why I feel the government has been fully engaged with the alien issue for many years, and has a tremendous amount of knowledge and experiences by now, if not direct interactions. However, this has had to remain top secret because it is the only way to retain a full advantage over competing governments who would like to achieve the same goals as the US. Thus, it is actually to the government's advantage to pretend that they are totally ignorant of any and all alien information. This is why the US government has consistently denied any knowledge of aliens, despite the obvious fact that they would have had many interactions with UFO or alien spacecraft activity.

I think the government's recent admission of some knowledge of UFO activity is an indication of an escalation in their attempt to gain more information for their alien program. In essence, I think there is an "alien race" occurring among superpower countries on Earth, similar to the "space race" we are all familiar with.

The other aspect to this discussion of aliens and why the government is keeping secrets, relates to the fact that I think the alien situation is already further down the road and more developed than most people can even realize. I believe the government is already aware of "alien genetics" and how we may already have "aliens" on this planet in our own countries. I believe we have these folks already working with or within our government and military. You read the chapter entitled "The Walk-In," right? I believe there are Americans who are very "different" from normal humans, and are very talented, who are working in alien programs within the government. My understanding is that people would have no imagination or comprehension for what is going on in that field of study, in addition to the advances and evidence already collected.

Notice I have not even mentioned Roswell except in reference. Whether or not the government recovered space craft from the Roswell incident is not relevant. First of all, any reverse engineering would not have yielded much useful information. Secondly, the information gained long after the Roswell incident is far more important and timely for our present reality.

I think what I am trying to say in all this is that the government knows way more about aliens than you can possibly imagine. I think they recognize the importance of a fruitful relationship with aliens, for both our own defense, and our aspirations for technological and political advancement and power.

The government is keeping it top secret not because they like to fool you, but because they MUST maintain a secure advantage over other superpowers. Remember, it's all a game, unfortunately. But that leads me to my next topic. What do the aliens think of all this, and what is their perspective?

First though, the US government's perspective is solely selfish in its desire to gain an advantage over everyone in the world in all ways possible. That is how governments think, and that is how humans think. But aliens do not think that way. The alien perspective is completely different.

Aliens view all of us as "humans." They do not feel there is an important distinguishment between different countries, groups, or races. They don't have a favoritism agenda. However, I am sure they are aware that some humans might be bad, some good, and some more dangerous than others. They would take all of those considerations into account.

However, the alien perspective would be to handle the humans in a logical beneficial way. Therefore, if certain government powers wish to engage with them, I am sure they would want to engage if it was safe to do so. All creatures of the Universe understand the concept of "mutual benefit." Aliens would understand this even better than humans. Thus, if there are security or stability concerns that engaging with a human government will benefit, then it is only logical to engage. Therefore, the aliens would engage.

However, my suspicion is that the aliens would be careful not to give any one political power group an unfair advantage over the others. The simple reason is that it would create instability on Earth. Humans have shown that when one group has a large advantage over another group, that more powerful group always uses their advantages to persecute and victimize weaker groups. Aliens know that they cannot trust Americans any more than they can trust Russians or the Chinese, or anyone else. Humans are humans, and humans are fairly undeveloped when it comes to self-discipline and maintaining morality. In fact, most humans would even admit there is no morality in government or war. Aliens are not about to give an unfair advantage to one party for this reason.

Therefore, much to the US government's dismay, they would likely be played by the aliens, or just pacified into thinking the aliens are responding favorably to them over others. The goal of the aliens would be to primarily maintain stability while continuing their own research and agendas.

Now, just for debate's sake, let us for a moment take the opposite side of this issue and assume the government actually knows nothing at all about aliens. How could this be and why? I think the answer would be that the aliens would have decided that it is too unsafe for the humans to know much about them. Perhaps the aliens made an assessment that a combination of very emotionally and mentally unstable humans, who also have a basic level of devastating weaponry, are not the type of folks you want to engage with.

The aliens would have decided it is better to keep a detached distance and just allow the humans to be intrigued as to what the odd unexplained spacecraft activity is all about. After all, let's face it, if the aliens wanted to continue operations as they have done, including abductions, they do not need any human involvement or official interaction to do this. They could just keep doing what they are doing, leaving almost no verifiable evidence of their existence. So that is the other side of the issue, and of course is possible until I can present you with verifiable evidence otherwise.

Regardless of that, I will maintain my more lengthy assertions in this chapter that the government already has full extensive knowledge of alien aircraft and aliens themselves. It is a more logical and likely conclusion don't you think?

CHAPTER EIGHT
Spaceships

L et's talk about UFOs. Actually, let's not. UFOs are "unidentified flying objects." This means they can actually be anything, or nothing, including balloons, optical illusions, traditional aircraft, experimental military aircraft, or a number of other aircraft or objects. Instead, let's talk about alien spacecraft. We shall define alien spacecraft, or spaceships, as flying machines that are not of human origin.

When many people think of alien spacecraft, they think about shape, size, material, and the beings flying inside it. However, by far the most important and interesting facet is PROPULSION. What powers these spacecraft? If we can answer that question, all the other questions and considerations we have about alien spacecraft would likely fall into place.

As with all topics involving aliens, it is hard to discuss spacecraft without bending the human understanding of reality and facts as they know them. Humans think within very narrow limitations, in very few dimensions of thinking. You will need to expand your thinking when considering propulsion for spacecraft.

I will start by saying that alien spacecraft have no propulsion. So, if you ask what secret advanced propulsion system must alien spacecraft be using, the answer is none. There is no propulsion. However, that is not exactly true either. There are some propulsion systems, depending on the craft and the use at the moment, but when it comes to zipping through space at incredible speeds, the answer is that there is no propulsion system.

How can this be? How can a spacecraft move through space with no propulsion system? Well first, let us consider what a propulsion system is. As the word suggests, a propulsion system is a structured system that PROPELS a spacecraft through space. That would infer that some type of system is PUSHING the craft through space. Is it a rocket? Fuel engines? Nuclear engines? Some kind of jets? What is pushing the craft through space? Nothing. Nothing is pushing it through space using methods as outlined above. Those won't work.

Consider for a moment any kind of propulsion technology you would like. Jet fuel, gas, oil, nuclear, or make up your own chemical fuel. The key word here is "fuel." Any propulsion system that requires "fuel" will not work because that means the craft would have to keep enough fuel onboard to travel across solar systems and galaxies, AND BACK AGAIN, without running out of fuel. Imagine the fuel storage the craft would have to have. The craft would have to be HUGE just to store the amount of fuel needed.

Additionally, propulsion systems that use fuel are simply not very efficient, and thus not powerful enough to provide the incredible speed and distance that is required for a spacecraft. Propulsion systems as we know them use fuel to burn, which then creates the energy to propel, and then the fuel waste is left behind.

For a propulsion system to be worthy of an interstellar spacecraft, there would have to be no limited storage required for the fuel, and there would have to be virtually no waste. In other words, it would have to be 100% efficient in every manner. That does not exist in our world, nor does it exist in our science. By definition, fuel requires storage and emits waste. That won't work for alien spacecraft that require 100% efficiency.

Most importantly, there is no propulsion system that is powerful enough to provide enough speed for a spacecraft to travel at incredible speeds, such as the speed of light and beyond. So, if there is no propulsion system that could work, and spacecraft have no propulsion system, then how do they move?

The complicated answer would be that spacecraft have multiple systems and methods for movement. This is where I might contradict myself and say that one of their many systems might be a mini-propulsion system for navigating within slow and tight spaces. A spacecraft may have jets that allow it to hover, land, and move right and left. That propulsion system will be very efficient beyond our technology, and only used in those specific circumstances.

For example, there are propulsion systems that use air, water, and chemicals. We all know about the steam engine, right? Imagine if you were able to create a chemical reaction that created the heat to turn the water to steam, which then powers an engine to thrust. We could talk about nuclear propulsion systems here also. That part is easy. Humans actually have the technology to figure out how to build a spacecraft that can navigate slowly, as well as back and forth.

The real issue is how does a spacecraft travel through space at incredible speeds to get from one solar system to another, from one star system to another? This cannot be done through propulsion as we know it. How can you move something without propulsion then? There are some ideas we can look at that are within the realm of human thinking.

For example, think of a magnet. Let's say I get my hands on a very powerful magnet. Next, I stand a distance away from the magnet while holding a paperclip. I let go of the paperclip. The paperclip then flies through the air and lands on the magnet. That paperclip just flew through the air without any propulsion system. The power was in the magnet, not the craft (paperclip).

What if I got us a bigger magnet and made the paper clip so huge that a person could sit inside it? We would then have a craft that is capable of flying through the air with no propulsion system. Also, keep in mind that a magnet can either pull something to it, or it can push things away. Regardless of whether the magnet is pulling or pushing, the craft would be moving.

How can I find a magnet big enough to pull or push a spacecraft incredible distances through space? Would my magnet have to be the size of a planet? Would that even work? I don't think so. We need to expand our thinking. Instead of a solid magnetic object, consider a magnetic field that acts the same as a large solid magnet. What if I can tap into a magnetic field to pull or push my craft? Better yet, what if I can CREATE my own magnetic field that I use to pull or push my craft? We might be onto something then?

Look, I am not a Physicist or Mathematician. I am not going to write equations out on a chalkboard for you. I also know some skeptics far smarter than me will be asking how such a magnet could work, and how it would relate to an electromagnetic field, and how such would be powered, and so forth. My answer is that the answer is within a method humans have not discovered yet. But don't worry, I am not doing a total cop-out here. The answer is going to be found by harnessing the incredible energy that already exists out in space within the Universe. The answer is NOT in a human's ability to generate the power themselves. The answer is in harnessing the power of the sun, stars, gravitational forces, and so on. That is the short-cut needed. It is very similar to waiting for a gust of wind to naturally pick you up by your wings, instead of wondering how you will generate wind on your own. The energy required is already there ready to be used. There will be more discussion about this in the next chapter.

But for now, let us move on to an additional different concept. We know light can travel quickly, right? What if I had a device that could convert objects into light particles? Think of a device that could scan a person's DNA for example. If you can scan a person's DNA to the most detailed level, you can then have the map of how every cell is constructed. What if I could then deconstruct that structure into light particles, and then moments later, reconstruct that structure back to how it was by using the "DNA map?" Basically, disassemble, travel as light particles, and then reassemble. This example will seem more far-fetched and difficult to grasp as possible reality. My goal though is to get you thinking outside the box. I promise you that humans will never figure out alien spacecraft as long as they think inside the box. It is beyond human comprehension. Therefore, if we know that up front, then our very first scientific assumption of how to advance, should be to think outside the box. Think in terms of science that we do not yet understand, but exists still the same.

Let us discuss another concept of space travel. Wormholes. What if we were able to either find wormholes, or create openings to wormholes where we needed them? Then, what if we were able to safely travel through them? Using a wormhole is like cheating space and time. It is a short-cut across space. Using a wormhole would mean that a spacecraft does not need to go fast at all. It might not even need much of a forward motion at all. Why would you need anything pushing or pulling your spacecraft at high speeds when you can enter a wormhole and be spit out at your destination? The wormhole spiraling affect would move you along. Some will argue that there still needs to be propulsion or movement inside the wormhole relative to the inside walls of the wormhole, but no, not really. Like electricity traveling through a wire, the wormhole would be pushing/pulling you with its natural state of being.

We already know wormholes exist, at least we think they do based upon our scientific theories. But even if we were to question the existence of wormholes, I submit to you that space is full of chaos. My proof is the existence of Black Holes. If a Black Hole can exist, then anything can exist. That is because Black Holes are the most chaotic thing in the Universe. Black Holes are nothing and everything all at the same time. That is chaos. Chaos is actually a source of power by the way. If you believe in the Big Bang theory, then you believe creation was born by a Singularity, or a Black Hole explosion. That is pretty chaotic. So what I mean by chaotic is that ANY GREAT AMAZING HUGE thing can happen in space. Anything.

The Universe and Space is always expanding. Therefore, it is never constant. Thus, it's chaotic. Space and time bends in ways that are always changing. This kind of chaos would allow for all kinds of weird things, such as wormholes and other anomalies. You can think of it as a portal in space, or you think of it as a huge tornado that you can enter on the ground, and then be pulled up into space to another place, with no propulsion or energy needed to be generated by you.

One of the morals of the story here, is this idea of CHAOS in space. Humans have a desperate need to figure everything out so that they can control everything. I personally might have hated math in school, but humans on a general philosophical level love math and science, because it allows them to feel that they KNOW FACTS, and thus can CONTROL their understanding of everything around them.

Even in the spirituality community you find gurus teaching people that there are no coincidences. They teach people that they can control everything with positive thoughts, and what they think about in their minds. We see this type of controlled thought within religion, and pretty much wherever you look in human society. Humans must know the absolute answer, and if they don't, they are determined that someday they will.

When I wrote my first book years ago called *The Hunter Equation*, I proposed in my book that a major element in the Universe was this notion of things being RANDOM. Just like it sounds, I proposed that some things just cannot be predicted or controlled. Many people absolutely hated this idea, and I was heavily trolled for suggesting it. How dare I suggest that humans do not have ultimate control of everything around them. Surely, if a human was smart enough in math and science, had strong enough thoughts of intention, and had a strong spiritual or religious compass, they could indeed have control, or have control in the sense that all of their outcomes were destined by fate. Well sorry, I just don't believe that. I didn't believe it back then, and I believe it even less now.

There is a random component to the Universe. My proof is that the Universe is always expanding, and therefore it is not constant. If it is not constant, then there are variables. If there are enough variables changing on a constant basis, then prediction is impossible. At that point, we have reached a level of chaos, which presents as a string of random events. I won't spend this book going down that rabbit hole, but we do have to establish that there is a random chaos in the Universe. This is what allows for an infinite amount of opportunities and options for utilizing space travel methods.

As I started out saying, I believe alien space travel is done using a variety of methods. These methods are employed depending upon the options available at the particular time and place, along with the objective and circumstances.

I will say this. The intelligent being who knows most about the Universe will be the being that has the most efficient method of space travel. I think traditional math and science as a way of developing space travel is very rudimentary. A human being smart enough to use math and science in order to use fuel to power a rocket up into space, would be considered very basic and low-level technology by more intelligent beings out there. I believe it would be equivalent to making tools out of rocks. It is using basic human intelligence to engineer a basic piece of equipment using basic methods and materials.

I assure you, a more advanced intelligent being will be working smarter, not working harder. They will be using "principles of the Universe" to achieve their objective. An example of a "principle of the Universe" would be gravity. That is something that we and all other beings would be familiar with. And since I brought it up, I would not be a bit surprised if an advanced species actually uses gravity in some way to achieve a type of travel, movement, or propulsion.

This is why I believe that any alien spacecraft already recovered by humans from crashes or such, is of limited use to humans. Any reverse engineering would only reveal the parts and pieces used in the small "scout crafts." The actual propulsion method would be either less advanced than in the larger spacecraft, and the parts and pieces do not tell you the method of travel. In other words, I believe the secret to space travel is within the basic principles of the Universe employed, and not within the parts and pieces of the actual aircraft. I think humans can reverse engineer alien spacecraft all they want, but will remain lost and confused as long as they do not understand the basic principles of the Universe being used to actually affect the long-distance travel.

You can give a monkey an airplane and sit them in the cockpit, but if the monkey does not understand the principles involved with reaching certain runway speeds and employing wing flaps and so forth, they won't be able to fly the plane. They would just rev the jet engines and push and pull the levers. The plane would never leave the ground. They would have to understand the basic principles of flying first. And believe me, aliens pretty much view humans as a bunch of monkeys at this point in evolution and development. Incidentally, it was a monkey that first went into space in a rocket before any human. How ironic (and appropriate).

Whatever the method used to power an alien spacecraft, it will be beyond Human science, math, and thinking. Therefore, thinking outside the box puts you ahead of most other humans when considering such questions. However, I believe it has to do with basic principles of the Universe. When humans learn the true answers of alien spacecraft, their reaction will be, "AHHHH DUH, YES OF COURSE."

With that said, while humans have it all wrong when it comes to propulsion, I believe humans might have a better grasp on the logistics involved with the types of alien spacecraft out there. There would be small craft that actually come from much larger spacecraft.

We have seen images of what we think are some small spacecraft. They tend to be either "saucers" or "Tic Tacs." These

84

craft seem to be very small. It is hard to imagine more than several beings being crammed into each craft. Most certainly, these beings did not travel alone across the galaxy in these tiny spacecraft. Can you imagine how cramped your legs would get? Never mind, don't answer that.

Also, I think it is important to consider the shape of an aircraft when we are trying to figure out a method of "propulsion," or how a spacecraft is able to move itself through space. Obviously, when considering both saucer shaped craft and Tic Tac shaped craft, one must observe that both of these shapes are very aerodynamic. I realize this observation will not win me the Nobel Prize for brilliance. But I think it is important to note in our book of evidential clues, that spacecraft seemingly must be aerodynamic in order to fly.

With that said, it should also be noted that neither the saucer nor Tic Tac shaped craft have wings. Thus, wings are not required. This tells us that "lift" is not required, as it is for all human aircraft other than rockets. I would also like to take note of another obvious trait of alien craft that could lead to deeper clues.

I don't think it should be underestimated the importance of the fact that the saucer craft are ROUND. I have always laid out my theories regarding other topics, that everything in the Universe is a circle, or round. The Earth is round, and the Universe is some form of round concave sphere, even if not perfectly round. Things go in circles and cycles. Pretty much everything in the Universe is based upon this concept of being round, or going in a circle.

I don't think we should think that alien spacecraft is round because aliens liked the appearance. I think we should fully assume that some alien spacecraft is round because that is part of the reason it can fly. Somehow, the craft being round might be part of how it moves through space. As I said before, the key to space flight will involve some universal basic concept that humans have yet to grasp. I would not be a bit surprised if it had something to do with the fact that everything in the Universe is round in some way. Thus, alien spacecraft are round saucer shaped. Humans should think about what happens when round objects spin at very high speeds. Perhaps that is a clue?

Anyway, the common-sense theory would be that these smaller craft we have been discussing are only "scout-craft" that are coming from a much larger starship. Humans can imagine a large starship like in *Star Trek* or some such thing. It would be large enough to be its own city. However, I propose that some starships might be large enough to "be" their own civilizations.

Again, think outside the box. Imagine a starship so large that it is more like a large asteroid or even "moon" that is able to use principles of the Universe to traverse the galaxy. The reason I think this is highly likely is because of the distances traveled. In order to travel great distances across galaxies, it would likely take many lifetimes of any organic being, even at very high rates of speed.

Therefore, traveling across the Universe for some civilizations would not be thought of as a mission that begins and ends. Rather, it would be thought of as a "lifestyle," or general way of life or life purpose for that civilization. Their life as they know it would only consist of their time on the starship. They would begin life there, and die there. Generations of living beings would just continue indefinitely, as they traverse the Universe.

Each generation would teach the younger generation all of the knowledge and skills needed to maintain the starship. They would also be taught the philosophy of why they are traveling, where they are traveling, and for what purpose they are traveling. Also taught, would be all the knowledge gained during the travels. In such a civilization, the knowledge base would be constantly changing based upon what they have encountered and learned during their travels across the Universe. In every sense of the word and concept, the children would see in their lifetimes new things that their parents could not even imagine. This is most true in a civilization that spends its existence traveling across the Universe.

Humans have never reported seeing such an incredible craft, but the human mind is easily able to imagine such a thing. If humans are eventually able to figure out how to achieve long distance and high-speed space travel, humans will likely propose a similar mission of having humans devote a lifetime to space travel, which even includes procreation and children on board.

But for now, I think the human imagination will mostly remain focused on what those flying saucers or Tic Tac shaped vehicles are doing zipping around in all directions above them. Still even more interesting than the spacecraft and how it navigates, is the question of who the pilots are. And thus, back to the primary focus of aliens themselves and their interactions with humans.

CHAPTER NINE
Abduction
Technologies

Many people wonder how an alien spacecraft can sneak up to a human target, somehow transport the human onto the aircraft, do testing and take samples, and then return the human back to where they were found; all of this without anyone seeing or the human remembering how it happened. It is one of the great mysteries of UFO and alien study, and one we are about to explore.

I suppose the best way for us to have this discussion is by walking through an abduction step by step. In the chapter "The Alien Agenda," I proposed the motive behind alien abductions. I talked about how aliens are studying humans to learn how humans possess the DNA genetic code, anatomy, and psychological conditioning, that allow humans to experience such intense emotions and sensations. Therefore, we have already set the scene as to WHY aliens would abduct humans. So now let us examine the actual abduction and how it happens.

Aliens select specific humans for study based upon different factors. One factor might be the ease with which they can be abducted. It is much easier to abduct a human camping in the forest, than it is to abduct a human from a crowded high-rise apartment building in the middle of New York City. Additionally, aliens may choose humans who they feel will handle the event with ease. They don't want humans who might be so traumatized that they become hysterical, violent, or psychologically damaged, such that they harm themselves or die. But most importantly of course, aliens will select humans with specific traits or attributes that they want to study or focus on more than others. These could be certain genetic markers, or could be psychological or behavioral traits. Basically, aliens screen and carefully select their subjects as any good scientific researchers would. After all, this is not a trial for medications where you want a random set of people. This is a more specific study where you want specific people whose bodies might provide more information.

Once they have selected their target, they go in for the abduction. I am sure this can happen many different ways depending on the circumstances, but for our purposes here, let us assume the aliens will be using a spacecraft. The spacecraft will be quite small and will need to reach the target position undetected. Alien spacecraft do not need loud engines with thrust, nor do they need wings or noisy blades. Alien spacecraft can be completely silent.

The spacecraft must also be completely stealthy and nearly invisible. I say "nearly invisible" because I do not think they become completely invisible. If they were invisible, we would never see them. There would be no alien UFOs. However, sightings are rare, and clearly the spacecraft can be very stealthy.

I believe all alien technology is based upon surprisingly simple concepts that are found in the Universe and in nature. The most ingenious things are surprisingly simple. Take the wheel for example. Very simple, yet earth shakingly brilliant and important. I believe spacecraft stealth technology might be based upon a simple little lizard creature called a chameleon. Again, I will avoid any obvious reference to our friends the Reptilians. Oops, ignore that reference I just made to our chameleon-like shape-shifting Reptilian alien friends.

A chameleon is a cute little lizard that can change colors and appearance based upon his immediate surrounding environment. This allows him to essentially become hidden or invisible. It is important

89

to note that the chameleon never becomes literally invisible. You can still see him. However, he blends into the immediate background, and is very hard to see unless you are specifically looking for him.

I believe alien spacecraft engage technology that does this exact same thing. The spacecraft never becomes literally invisible. However, the craft can scan its surrounding environment from all angles, and can then project an exact match onto its outer skin of the spacecraft. It is so sophisticated, that it is able to project a perfect match, even though the image it projects might differ around different sides of the spacecraft.

For example, if there is darkness and essentially black from one angle, that angle of the craft will be black on the outer skin. But if from another angle, you can see trees in the background, then that side of the craft will project those exact trees onto the outer skin of the craft.

The spacecraft turns itself into a perfect chameleon to match its immediate background surroundings. If you are standing at a distance from the spacecraft, you won't see it. It is not invisible, but you will not see it because it perfectly matches the background surrounding it. It is basically playing an optical illusion on your sight and mind so that you don't see the spacecraft.

However, like a chameleon, if you looked very closely and knew what you were looking for, you would of course see that something was there. It might appear as some kind of distortion, or you might sense something is wrong with the placement and distance of the image you are seeing. However, the stealth technique will be good enough to create an illusion of invisibility most of the time in order to accomplish the mission at hand.

The next issue would be getting the human target into the spacecraft. We are going to assume a few logical and common-sense things. First, we will assume that aliens do not come into your bedroom and conduct testing on you there. I can tell you from my

90

own potential abduction incident, that I felt and was convinced, that NOBODY had been in my bedroom except myself. We can also say it would not be practical for aliens to risk being seen in your bedroom if others are in the same house or building. Additionally, most abduction stories indicate that the person was in a foreign environment during the abduction, such as a spacecraft or laboratory, and not in their own home or setting.

So, there will be no aliens coming to you in your bedroom. I think we can also assume there will be no aliens walking you down hallways, steps, and walkways, in order to escort you up some stairs into their spacecraft. That obviously won't work either. In my own abduction case, it was in the middle of winter, freezing cold outside, and there was no way I ever stepped foot outside. Additionally, there were no footprints outside the next morning.

This leaves us with the prospect that aliens somehow are able to get a human from their home environment, and directly transport them onto the spacecraft in a fairly seamless manner. This is where we start hypothesizing. Do they have some kind of transporter device that allows them to break you down into particles and then put you back together again on the other end? Maybe.

Another idea is that aliens use some kind of energy field as a tractor beam of sorts. We have heard abduction accounts where the person was standing below a spacecraft that was hovering above them, when all of a sudden they saw a beam of light, and then remember nothing else. This might suggest they were taken into the craft by a tractor beam of some sort.

I believe this is very possible through the use of various energy fields. Whether it be some kind of magnetic field, or electromagnetic field, or perhaps some kind of energy field humans have not discovered yet, it would be an effective way to reach out and grab something. Incidentally, I believe the use of energy fields also might tie into how spacecraft travel and navigate, as I referred to in the previous chapter. If humans discover one of the keys to this technology, many other doors will open more quickly after that.

The self-creation of energy fields would be necessary in the creation or opening of wormholes and other methods of high-speed space travel. Physicists will tell you that using energy fields to create wormholes and other similar things would be impossible because of Maxwell's equations. Maxwell's equations indicate a basic premise that the energy within a given energy field is equal to the energy it took to create the energy field. This suggests a zero-sum game. In other words, if a wormhole can only be opened by a huge unearthly amount of energy, that would mean humans would have to actually create that amount of energy themselves first. This would deem the task practically impossible. This is what they say anyway.

While I cannot argue with the physics and math involved, and certainly won't argue with Mr. Maxwell, I do take issue with the final conclusion. I do not believe the task is impossible, because I believe the steps of logic are not correct. The best way for me to express my point is to give an analogy as example. Please bear with me as we are now deep inside the weeds and lost in the woods down a deep rabbit hole. I'll get us out eventually, don't worry.

Let us take the science of flying for example. Once upon a time we thought flying was impossible. Gravity was given as the absolute proof as to why flying up in the sky would be impossible. People could show you gravitational equations if you doubted this conclusion that flying would be impossible. A human or machine cannot get into the air due to gravity, so they said. Period. Science. Physics. Period.

Well, while it is true that gravity exists and the equations for gravity exist, the conclusion that it meant flying was impossible was certainly very wrong. The reason the conclusion was wrong is because those total believers in gravity failed to take into account the principle of "lift."

You can imagine people staring up at birds and seeing them fly around in the sky. Those people would have thought how gravity makes it impossible to fly up in the sky. Perhaps people thought birds had special powers, or maybe they could fly because they were so tiny. Certainly, the laws of gravity would forever prevent humans and large heavy machines from flying in the air.

But no. Anything can fly in the air if they utilize the concept of "lift." If I have wings and some wind, I can fly. That is lift. What a wonderful principle that totally violates the laws of gravity, except it doesn't violate the laws of gravity. If I lose my lift, gravity will indeed take me to the ground in a hurry, and the landing won't be gentle. Thus, the laws of gravity remain intact. But lift allows me to cheat gravity by using the wind and air to stay in the air. I can rely on the wind for this, or I can use engines to create the forward motion for the air needed for lift. Of course, the heavier the item to fly, the more lift needed. In human airplane terms, that means a combination of larger wings and larger engines for more thrust.

My whole point is that those who thought gravity would prevent anyone from flying, did not take into consideration that lift would allow people to circumvent the conclusion that people couldn't fly. I am simply suggesting the same thing here. Even though Maxwell's equations "prove" that humans cannot generate enough energy to create the amount of energy needed for powerful energy fields or wormhole space travel, that does not mean that humans cannot find this massive energy elsewhere. I mentioned potential sources of incredible energy in the previous chapter.

I am suggesting that humans DON'T need to generate massive amounts of energy themselves to create advanced alien technology. Like the concept of "lift," I believe aliens have found principles that circumvent the usual conclusions of physics. Aliens do not generate massive energy to open wormholes or create energy fields. Instead, aliens utilize the nature resources around them to use and take advantage of massive sources of energy that naturally exist already.

To carry on with my analogy, it would be equivalent to how a person can fly with no engines at all if they use the wind on a windy day. You just have to know how to utilize the natural wind. When I traveled in Brazil, I watched these men hand gliding high above the city by launching themselves (running) off a steep cliff hillside into the wind. It looked horrifying, but they were able to get enough lift to do it without any mechanized engines. They had found the perfect location with the perfect launch pad, on the perfect day with enough wind coming at them in the correct direction. They were utilizing what nature was providing for free and naturally.

Aliens use the same philosophy and science when generating enough energy to power an energy field, or create enough power to travel at the speed of light. Aliens have learned how to tap into massive amounts of energy so that they don't have to create it themselves. They can use these techniques for spacecraft thrust and power, or for very strong and effective energy fields for moving objects and people.

They can use this technology for abducting humans onto a spacecraft with an energy field type tractor beam. Phew. And here we are back outside the rabbit hole again. I told you I would get you back out. Let us continue on our regularly scheduled discussion now after that winding detour.

The conclusion I am trying to suggest and support is that aliens can easily access technology that can move their human target from the human's bedroom or wherever, onto the spacecraft without ever leaving the spacecraft. Once in the spacecraft, the human is already sedated. The sedation would happen at the beginning of the transporter process. The energy field used to transport the human would contain the sedation agent.

Safely on board the spacecraft and sedated, the testing and samples would be done on the human, most likely very quickly and efficiently, while providing great care not to damage the human. There are accounts of people waking up from the sedation and seeing the aliens. I'm sure the aliens were never thrilled when their sedation failed. However, they did not want to over-sedate and harm the humans either. Nobody is perfect, not even aliens.

Once the testing is done and any samples retrieved, the human would be transported back to the place where they were found. There would be the anti-sedation agent contained within the energy field that transported the human back home. With any luck, the human would be confused but not think much of the situation, and simply go to bed. The next day they might sense from their inner feelings that something odd happened, but would disregard it. Even if a human were to wake up the next morning and feel they were abducted by aliens, they would fully assume they ate something bad the night before, or maybe just needs a nap or vacation. Any slight memories or suspicions would usually be dismissed.

Of course, what changes this dynamic is if the human remembers anything clearly, or if they have any physical evidence that is strange. For example, when you wake up with a puncture wound on your thumb that was not there when you went to bed, that is a piece of evidence that is hard to dismiss.

The abduction scenario outlined above is not the easiest and most ideal scenario for aliens. That is why I outlined it that way. Obviously, the easiest abductions will be with humans who are alone out in the wilderness camping. Anyone can pull off an abduction under those conditions. I suggested a more complicated scenario as a way of suggesting that abductions can be done in many different settings, and do not require total isolation. It is for this reason that I believe many more people are abducted than is realized or traditionally believed.

There is a huge number of people reading this who feel deep inside they also have been abducted. They might not have admitted it to anyone, or even to themselves. To those people I say, you are not

95

alone. We are not alone.

CHAPTER TEN

Why Don't Aliens Help Us?

I get asked a lot why I think aliens do not help humans with their problems. For example, why don't aliens help heal the Earth? Why don't aliens help cure disease? Why don't aliens help humans evolve technologically? If aliens are so benevolent, then why don't they help humans end suffering and solve our most pressing problems?

Don't people ask the same about God? If God is an all-loving God, and we pray and do all the right things, then why does God allow humans to suffer? The fact that God allows good people to suffer does not seem to sway the most religious among us from still believing in God, and believing that God is good.

I will let those more qualified than me answer the questions of why God allows suffering, or perhaps that is for another book. Instead, I will share some thoughts on why I think aliens allow the same suffering as God allows, without stepping in to help humans by using aliens' vast advanced technologies and knowledge.

Why don't aliens help humans with their problems? The answer is embarrassingly simple. Why would aliens help solve a problem that humans intentionally created and/or fail to take any action to solve themselves? Almost all human problems are self-inflicted. Whether it be environmental problems due to pollution or climate change, disease, malnutrition, violence, starvation, homelessness, weapons, or whatever else you can think of, all of the problems are caused by humans themselves. Worse yet is the fact that even when humans fully see the problem, and know of solutions, humans still fail to engage with the solutions to fix the problem.

Before we go further, let me just quickly preface my comments by saying that I am not trying to judge people's opinions about matters involving society or politics. Many human problems are not solved because humans have different opinions and preferences as to how to deal with them. My aim with this discussion is simply to look at things from a logical point of view as it relates to how aliens may view the situation.

Let us continue and explore some of the questions, issues, and concerns many people have regarding problems humans have, which aliens with superior technologies might be able to solve. It really comes down to things that cause human suffering, doesn't it? That is what really matters. The Earth having issues with many decades of pollution has affected our atmosphere, which has affected our weather. We have wild extreme weather that causes floods, draughts, and fires, more so than in past history. Science indicates this is caused by climate change, which was caused by pollution that damaged the ozone layer.

Pollution is something that humans caused, and is something humans can prevent. Humans can choose to stop polluting if they really wanted to, but they don't. The reasons are political and psychological. We do not need to go into all of them. But the fact remains that humans can stop pollution if they chose to. They choose not to. Why would aliens help humans solve a problem that humans have chosen to cause, and have chosen not to solve?

If your child took a sledgehammer to their bicycle, and then asked you to help them with their broken bicycle, what would you do? Would you say, "Hey, no problem, I know you just destroyed it on purpose, but I would love to give my money and time to fix it for you." Or, would you say, "You chose to break it, you fix it yourself or

98

go without." I know what my parents would have said to me. Maybe others out there had it much easier than me, but I suspect most of you would have gone without their bicycle like I would have.

Why would aliens help humans fix a problem that humans caused and don't care to use their solutions to fix it? Aliens would assume that humans either wanted it broken, or have another plan to fix it that they don't understand. They would leave us to it. Remember, aliens would think very logically because that is how they became so technologically advanced. Through logical intelligent thought and cooperation is how they became advanced.

What about disease? Why don't aliens provide us with treatments and cures for diseases? Well first of all, many diseases are caused by humans themselves. Humans allow themselves to live in toxic environments that make them sick. Humans use chemicals in their living environments that poison their air, water, and food. Humans allow their foods to be poisoned if it decreases the cost of the food, and the poison seems fairly safe over the short-term. Humans consume illicit drugs, smoke, and drink alcohol, all of which are intentional self-poisonings.

What's worse than that, is humans hesitate in producing medicines that would cure their diseases. Many humans don't believe in science, don't trust science, and don't trust the researchers and doctors who use science to create cures. But that is actually understandable to a degree. For much of human history, humans have been manipulated by those promising miraculous cures or outcomes, only to realize they were lies, or even harmful treatments. Humans have been lied to by their political leaders so often that they no longer believe a thing they are told.

It has gotten to the point that if humans were facing a deadly plague, and were offered a medicinal cure that worked magically well, many humans would assume it is a lie, and would refuse to take the treatment. Some humans would rather die of the disease than accept a treatment that they don't trust from people they don't trust. I know it sounds insane and illogical, but it could happen!

And before you start thinking humans are just plain stupid, again remember that humans respond this way because of all the lies they have been subjected to in the past by corrupt and dubious leaders, and people just trying to profit by any means possible, even if that means making false claims.

We can also say that many humans profit by not allowing legitimate cures to come to market. If a corporation earns all of its profits from selling a cancer treatment, why would it allow a cancer cure to come to market? A cure would put the corporation selling the treatment out of business. Thus, that corporation will actually use its financial and political power to stop any cure from coming to market. That is logical. It is doing what is best to maintain its profits. However, allowing such a system to exist is totally illogical, since that system can result in blocking cures that can change all of humanity for the good.

An alien society would examine this and naturally assume that humans like, and want, disease, because it's profitable to them. After all, humans cause most of the disease themselves, and then they have a system that potentially blocks any cures for the disease. They see that humans actually make profits from disease. Why would aliens not logically assume that humans want and need disease for the economic system they have intentionally built? Aliens would not want to interfere with our societal and economic systems that humans seem to depend on and desire.

Besides, even if aliens provided a medical treatment cure for our diseases, humans would not accept it or use it. Humans would not trust the aliens or the science behind the cures given. Humans would be convinced it is a trick to poison them or control them somehow. Humans would refuse any actual help offered in many cases. So again, why help the humans if they would not even accept the help if it was offered?

Based upon the previous discussions we just had, I think you get the idea. I don't think we need to discuss other problems such as homelessness, addiction, or things like that, which can obviously be solved, but humans don't want to because it would violate their current economic, political, and societal systems. Humans built their society so that these problems can exist and won't be solved. Humans must have done this on purpose. It is only logical, right?

Okay, I have beaten this subject to death. Nobody wants to hear more about what humans have caused and refuse to solve. It annoys people. So, I'll stop. Instead, let us look at something more feasible that maybe aliens could help humans with.

Why don't aliens help humans develop more advanced technology? Unlike the prior issues that humans cause and refuse to fix, technology is a totally different discussion. Humans actually genuinely want to develop more advanced technology, and humans put a tremendous amount of sincere effort into trying to do this. Certainly, aliens would help humans with technology since humans seem to truly want this, and put forth all their effort into developing it, right?

Well, no. Let's make that an emphatic NO. But come on! Sure, aliens might not want to help us with things we are unwilling to help ourselves with, but why not help us with things we are making a real effort to accomplish? I am sure some of you might see the potential problem. If humans are so irresponsible with many of their existing technologies, then imagine how irresponsible humans would be with even greater technologies.

Why would aliens provide humans with technologies that would most certainly result in humans using the technology to either harm other humans, harm the Earth, or cause self-inflicted wounds to themselves? If an alien gives a human a laser zapper gun that can immediately remove debris that covers a human trapped and dying in fallen debris, then that sounds great and helpful, right? Well yeah, except for the fact that it would take about five minutes for that lifesaving zapper gun to be turned into a weapon and used on other humans to zap them out of existence. So even though that alien zapper gun would be an amazing device to save humans who are in building collapses, or trapped in car wrecks, aliens cannot allow humans to have that technology. It does not take a genius to know with certainty that the humans would weaponize that technology and cause themselves and their planet further harm. So, sorry, no technology for you! Of course, we hope someday this might change. I truly believe that if aliens were convinced that humans would use technology for the greater good of the Universe, they would very likely share. It is the logical thing to do. There is no greed in a world of logic because greed is not logical.

I know all of this seems very cynical. It is cynical, my apologies. But it's the truth. I am trying to answer the questions as truthfully and honestly as possible. I also realize that some humans think and react very differently from others. Additionally, I believe humans can evolve into a place where they are more responsible and able to solve their own problems.

I do not think we should place ourselves in a mindset that has us depending on aliens to solve our problems. I truly believe that humans can solve all of their own problems if they decide to. My absolute proof of this is the fact that humans were able to cause their own problems. If a human is able to dig a deep hole, I believe they can use the same shovels, dirt, and expertise to fill the hole back in. The problem is that human society was designed to dig deep holes, but not designed to fill them back in. But that too can be changed.

So, why don't aliens help us? Well, because we caused our own problems, don't want to solve them, and would not accept help even if it was offered. But the real answer is that aliens don't help humans because humans need to learn to help themselves. This is the only way humans can truly evolve into a higher being. There are no shortcuts, and aliens know this already because they likely lived it themselves thousands of years before us. So let our work begin.

CHAPTER ELEVEN

Who Is More Afraid
Of Whom?

When I was little, I spent a lot of time in the woods alone. By "little" I mean starting at age six. So yes, I was a six-year-old boy roaming around the forest with no supervision. Where were my parents you ask? Well, my father had vanished when I was three, and my mother was always either working or taking care of our trailer home that sat in a rural area of New England at the forest's edge. So, I just roamed about, and since I always managed to make it back in time for dinner, my mother figured all was well, and it was.

However, at such a young age I had been exposed to all the fairy tale stories of animals and monsters in the woods. My psychology was such that if I saw a fox or coyote, I would fully assume it was going to try and eat me. I was terrified of most animals. I was even scared of deer.

Eventually though, I came to realize that animals were far more afraid of me than I was of them. In the rare instances when I would come across a fox or deer, they would immediately run away from me as fast as they could. Why were these animals I was so afraid of, running away from ME in such fear? How can they be scared of me when I am scared of them? Who is more afraid of whom?

Well apparently, much to my surprise the animals were much more afraid of me than I was of them. This caused me to lose my fear of the animals. I knew that if I came upon one, it would run from me, and therefore I had nothing to worry about. This fascinated me though, because I was certain that in a "cage match" most of these animals could beat me. Deer were so much bigger and stronger than me. Certainly, a deer could kill me easily. And a fox and coyote could easily kill me if it got me by the neck. So why would these animals fear me when they could clearly take me out much more easily than I could take them out?

Obviously, I quickly grew to realize that humans often had weapons that could be used on the animals. I supposed it only takes a fox getting shot at once, for the fox to realize that humans are very dangerous and not to be messed with. Therefore, the dynamics were more about what humans would do to you, rather than how strong or fierce an actual human was. When compared to wild animals, humans are quite fragile and weak creatures. However, they come bearing devasting weapons, and humans have no hesitation in using such weapons.

How might the dynamics be similar or different between humans and aliens? Like myself as a child, humans have been mentally conditioned to fear aliens. Aliens are "monsters" who look different and have advanced powers to travel through space. Aliens must be very scary and should be feared, yes?

Additionally, aliens have much greater and more powerful technologies than humans. So not only are aliens "unknown" and look different or scary, but they also must have powerful weapons. So, what is there NOT to fear about aliens? Aliens are scary all around and thus humans should fear them?

I describe all of this from the fear-based perspective of humans. Humans always view everything from the lens of fear. However, what happens if we apply observation and logic to the equation? Have we ever seen an alien shoot at, or eat, a human, like humans do to animals? Have you ever seen an alien hunting in the forest hoping to kill a human and drag it out of the forest to be cut up and stuffed into a freezer for food? Have you seen aliens shooting humans with rifles for no other reason than sport?

If aliens have the ability to build amazing spaceships and travel across the Universe, then surely they have the ability to harm humans if they so desired, right? Yet we have not seen this happen. Animals run from humans because animals have seen humans do bad things to them and other animals. Humans would run from aliens, even though humans have not seen aliens do bad things to them or to other humans. Animals are being logical by running from humans, but humans are being irrational by running from aliens.

Now let's flip the script. Are aliens afraid of humans? If humans are so afraid of aliens, then it must mean that aliens are more superior and more dangerous than humans? If true, then there would be no reason for aliens to run from humans. Do you think aliens would run from humans? It makes me think of the more powerful large deer running from me when I was a little child. The deer was so much larger and more powerful than me, yet it seemed afraid and would run from me. Would aliens run from me as well, even though they are more powerful?

It is not supposed to work this way. Humans are supposed to be afraid of aliens, not the other way around. Or was that just artificial human conditioning? Are humans afraid of aliens for reasons of irrational conditioning, or are humans afraid of aliens for logical good reasons?

Some say that humans should be very afraid of aliens because they have advanced technology that can destroy us. Yes, but why is it that no alien has used this technology to wipe out humans or harm them yet? While humans never thought twice about using weapons to harm others, it seems aliens have not used their technologies to harm humans.

I think if the shoe was on the other foot and humans had incredible advanced technology as aliens do, humans would have used this

106

technology to harm others by now, even though aliens in this situation have not. Humans have a history of carnage. Humans develop technology, and then use it against other people, or other living creatures. A human's first thought when seeing something interesting is usually, "Wow that would make a great weapon," or "Wow, I might be able to really profit from this." That is how humans have typically thought throughout history.

But let's get back to the question of whether aliens are afraid of humans or not. Why wouldn't they be? Aliens would have observed humans long enough to see all of the history and behaviors I mentioned above. Aliens would clearly see that humans have a history of always weaponizing technology. Aliens would clearly see that humans always react out of fear, and often that reaction is violent, irrational, and without much contemplation. Humans can be quite scary creatures.

Aliens are very possibly terrified of humans for this reason. It does not matter if aliens have more advanced technology or are smarter than humans. In another analogy, it does not matter if humans are more technologically advanced and smarter than lions. Lions can still attack and eat you. Sometimes technology and intellect matter not. Sometimes what matters more is how violent and fierce the BEHAVIOR is. It would make sense that aliens might view humans in a very similar way to how humans view lions. Aliens know they are superior, but that does not make humans any less scary or dangerous to them.

This might explain why aliens are very hard to find. Aliens might not want to be found by humans. It would be dangerous to just walk up to a human, just like it would be dangerous to walk up to a lion. If a human is camping out in the wilderness, that human actually hopes and prays that a lion will not find them. I'm sure aliens feel the same way about humans.

If there are aliens on Mars, the moon, or any other places, I am sure they are hoping that humans never find them. I bet aliens take great care to keep their locations concealed from humans. If aliens are nearby, such as on Earth or the moon, they would be in places where humans won't find them. Aliens might hide on the dark side of the moon that humans can never see, or deep in the dark depths of our oceans, or underground within the Earth. There are some theories that the moon itself is an artificial alien base, and the base is located within the moon, leaving the surface of the moon completely barren. And we have not even discussed Mars yet.

The point is that wherever aliens may be, they are hiding. Beings only hide when they are concerned for their safety. Thus, logic tells us that aliens are concerned for their safety. Yes, they are more advanced than humans, but like the lion, humans can still kill.

What do you suppose would happen if humans found an alien base within Earth, whether it be in the ocean or underground? Would the first reaction of humans be to amass a huge military force and then go in for the attack? Would humans want to immediately capture or kill any aliens? Or would humans knock on the front door with some homemade lasagna as a way of welcoming new neighbors? I have a pretty good hunch it would be the former and not the latter.

What would happen if humans discovered that aliens were based on or within the moon? Would humans put together a huge space force so they could go and conquer the moon? It sounds crazy, but there is too much potential truth in it as well. It would be completely reasonable and logical for any aliens to fully assume that humans would attempt to invade and attack any alien base they discovered. It is for this reason that aliens would fear humans and take all precautions necessary to conceal their locations.

Is it possible that alien children go to bed each night reading scary fairy tales about savage humans? Well, it is possible. I personally do not think aliens have the mindset of demonizing others out of fear like humans do. That is more of a fear-based human trait. Aliens would have more of a logical based mindset. Aliens might think of humans as curious interesting creatures, but be very cautious of them. Isn't that the same way humans think of lions?

So I ask again, who is more afraid of whom? Well, I suppose both humans and aliens are afraid of each other, is the truth of the matter. However, one of those groups has reasonable logical reason to be afraid, while the other one does not. I will leave it for each person to decide which group is which.

CHAPTER TWELVE
Our Sisters
And Brothers

Have you ever wondered what it's like for those people who live their lives thinking they are an only child, but then find out later on in life that they have a long-lost brother or sister they never knew about? It must be mind-blowing. Perhaps those people felt something all along, but could never put their finger on it or substantiate it. And once they find out, they have to readjust their mind to the idea that they are not alone. They actually have family they never thought they had. What a mind-bending crazy wonderful blessing that must be.

Well, deep within me I feel that same feeling that I cannot put my finger on or fully substantiate. I believe humanity here on Earth has extended family they are not aware of. I do not think this is the only "Earth," and I do not think everyone on Earth are the only humans in the Universe.

The Universe is so large and vast, with almost an infinite number of planets. I refuse to believe that Earth is a one-off, and that all the humans in the entire Universe are only located on this one planet. This kind of assumption is not logical and therefore does not make sense.

Certainly, there is another planet very similar to Earth somewhere in the Universe, and on that planet are other humans. Or perhaps humans are located on a planet very different from Earth. Regardless of how you want to parse words, I believe there are other humans out there somewhere.

Imagine meeting them. What are they like? Are they the same as humans on Earth? Do they have the same societal systems? I doubt it. Similar to that cousin who you are supposedly related to, but is NOTHING like you, I feel there might be a similar situation in my suggested scenario as well.

I believe our sisters, brothers, cousins, or however you want to refer to them, would have the same anatomy as our humans here, but would have a totally different psychology. I say this because much of human psychology was formed through environmental pressures, conditioning, but also random societal events. Human structures on Earth are based mostly on a hierarchical structure of some humans being more powerful and important than other humans. This has created a society where the mass majority of humans are actually repressed. The mass majority of humans on Earth struggle in some way, and go without everything they need and want, while other humans are afforded the luxury of having anything they want, even if they don't need it.

Humans on Earth have become fully accepting of our societal structure, overwhelmingly support it, and act to continue it indefinitely. I believe this psychology is more of a conditioned response rather than a genetic response. Genetically, humans tend to be quite selfish and greedy. Humans always want things for themselves. If this is the case, then how did these same humans become conditioned to live under a societal system where they usually cannot have what they want, but those who are privileged can?

It would not be a natural logical response for humans to accept this kind of system. Therefore, the logical conclusion is that humans were conditioned to accept this system, even though it runs against their nature. To explain how this happened and why it happened, would require another book just on this subject. So, I am not going to go there now. I'm sorry and you're welcome.

But with that said, I believe the societies on other human planets

111

would be different. If there are multiple human planets, we would likely see a variety of societal structures. For example, one human planet might have a society that is more equal in terms of all humans receiving their maximum equal share of resources. This would be more in line with the idea of all humans being selfish and greedy enough, that they would not accept being cheated out of their fair share of resources.

But we also might find some other human planets to have societies similar to ours in terms of random events that precipitated psychological conditioning that rendered unexpected societal structures. Perhaps other societies have humans where they live in a very basic and primitive way with no technology. Maybe there was no motivation to develop technology because the humans were satisfied living alongside nature. They may have no technology, but they would also have no pollution and other negative bi-products of a technologically advanced society. Perhaps they live happier lives even without technology?

We might find other human planets are much more technologically advanced than our Earth. Perhaps those humans focused fully on education and development rather than consumption. Those are the humans I want to focus on for the rest of this chapter. I suggest to you that there are humans out there in the Universe that are far more advanced than the humans on Earth. I would suggest to you that those humans might have the capability for high speed deep-space travel. It might be those humans who find Earth someday, and stop by for a visit, just like that weird cousin you don't know well or never met, all of a sudden showing up at your door unannounced because they are family.

I believe it could happen. So, if a large amazing spaceship landed on Earth, and out stepped humans looking exactly like us, what would we think? What would we do? My guess is that we would have a very similar look on our face as you would if that weird cousin showed up at your door unannounced. We would be confused, shocked, and probably annoyed.

Who are these humans? How did they get such an amazing spacecraft? Where are they from? Why are they human? How come these humans are so much more advanced and "successful" than we are? Humans on Earth would be very suspicious and annoyed indeed. But I think some of us would also be intrigued and even thrilled that we had relatives. I mean think about it. Would you rather see familiar looking humans stepping off that large spacecraft, or would you rather see giant two-headed space monsters stepping off that spacecraft? Maybe the weird cousins are not so bad after all?

The meeting would be awkward for sure. I'm sure there would be some language problems as well. But it would be an interesting meeting indeed. There would be a lot of questions from both parties. One of the first questions for you to consider is whether or not you would consider them to be "aliens." Yes, they are human, but they are not from Earth. Thus, I suggest they would be aliens indeed. This is where I again get to remind you to keep a very open mind as to what aliens will turn out to be, and what to expect and not to expect. What we think of as aliens might not be what we discover.

Any way you slice it, these humans from another planet would be considered aliens. We already call some Earth humans aliens today. In the USA, immigrants from another country are often called aliens, as a technical immigration term for someone who is not an American citizen. Yes, we call them aliens. Kind of a derogatory term if you really think about it, since they do actually live here on Earth. In addition, our new humans from a different planet would be referred to as aliens as well.

How would our immigration system handle these aliens from another planet? Would they be considered immigrants? Would they have arrived legally or illegally? Would they be granted special status because they are humans? Does species, race, skin color, and so forth make a difference in now we handle immigrants and aliens? I'm just full of questions today, but inquiring minds want to know.

I mention all this because it can get confusing how we label "people." Are humans from other planets considered "people," while aliens from other planets are considered "aliens?" Or, are they considered monsters if they look big and scary? Does how a being look change how we label them, even though they all would be coming from a different planet or place?

I am raising these questions because humans on Earth will need to decide how they are going to treat aliens from other planets when they arrive. They may already be here of course. Will aliens already here be given special status? What if a human is part alien genetically? What if a human has an alien consciousness within them? What will their classification and status be? How will everyone be treated? Will it matter what type of human, color of skin, or whether they have big eyes or not, determine their immigration status or label?

I suspect some of the answers to these questions are precisely why aliens have not dared interact freely and openly with humans on Earth yet. Humans on Earth are not ready yet. To be ready, they would have to come up with satisfactory and compassionate answers to all the questions posed above.

I think humans on Earth can get to that point eventually. I have faith. It can be fun to have extended family. Yes, they might end up being different from us that are already here on Earth, but they are still family and we can find things in common with them. Maybe if we know there are other humans out there on other planets, we won't feel so alone. Maybe it could give us hope that there are other places we could go and live if we needed. But that idea only works if the humans here are willing to let those humans from other planets come here and live here if needed. It is just something I pose for consideration and contemplation.

Personally, I feel they are out there. It is not likely we will run into

114

them, but that does not change the idea of them being out there, somewhere. I hope they are doing well. The struggle is real. I wish them the best, as I wish all of us the best.

CHAPTER THIRTEEN
Alien Society

Many people wonder what alien society must be like. The first response should always be that it depends on what species of aliens you are talking about. I have done a lot of over generalizing and alien stereotyping in this book. I apologize to all alien species and cultures for doing this. However, it is necessary to limit the scope of conversation and keep things somewhat simple, in order to have a meaningful discussion of the basic principles involved in alien thinking, technology, and life.

Just like humans have many cultures within their species, aliens have different cultures within their species as well, and there are many different species of aliens in addition. So, to stereotype and jump to standard assumptions of alien life is somewhat "human," and offensive to aliens, as it would be to humans. With that said, and that disclosure and apology made, I am going to focus our vision and image of aliens around the species of aliens who likely surround Earth most closely. That seems like the reasonable and relevant thing to do. So onward we go.

Just so you know I am not pulling random thoughts out of the air, as if I was writing some kind of science fiction romance novel, I am going to base this discussion on some basic principles that I am hoping you all find plausible and logical. They are as follows:

1. As evidenced by their superior technology and scientific prowess, aliens are very logical in their thought, and based in a world of science, technology, and development.
2. As evidenced by their apparent space travel, along with interest in observing humans, in addition to conducting abductions to

further their studies, aliens are very curious creatures who value research more than most other pursuits.
3. As evidenced by the fact that aliens have not waged any attacks, wars, or violent aggressions toward humans, it is logical to assume that the current aliens near Earth are essentially a peaceful and benevolent species.

Rather than continue constructing a long list of assumptions (which I could do), I think we will keep it simple and run with those three assumptions above. They are enough for us to draw many likely conclusions about alien culture.

The fact that aliens possess advanced technology and do not seem to use it recklessly, tells us that alien society is based upon logical thinking, science, and cooperation. Like any species and any planet civilization, they would have limited resources to draw from, and they clearly are highly efficient at using those resources. It is fair to say that "efficiency" is a bi-product of logical thinking.

Aliens make sound decisions based upon careful observation, facts, and analysis. They would not make snap decisions based upon emotion. Everything is very well thought out and executed. Their choices and missions would be based upon sound reasoning, science, and highly probable and predictable outcomes.

Their "hierarchy" would be based upon those individuals with the most experience, skill, talent, and wisdom. Aliens are trying to use all of their resources in the most efficient way in order to gain the most useful and bountiful results from their objectives and missions. If you are able to think with total logic, you are able to see more clearly how aliens think and structure their society.

Every individual within their society would be considered a valuable resource. Their society is not unlike a very well-run Human Resources Department on Earth. A good Human Resources Department takes into account all of the people they must utilize, and then places those people in the positions in which they are likely to have the most success, and thus benefit the business the most. Additionally, a good Human Resources Department has programs to support and encourage their people so that they can become even more productive. I know many of you in the corporate world are laughing as you read this because in REALITY, this is not how most Human Resource Departments operate. But this is how they SHOULD operate, ideally.

In alien society, this is how they operate, but in a more extended advanced way. Individuals would be given total support to become the best they can be at whatever their greatest potential might be. The greater the individuals, the greater their ultimate contributions will be. The greater number of great contributions there are, the more advanced the society and their technology will become. Again, their societal goal is based upon technology and research.

Thus, in alien society there is no incentive or compulsion toward amassing more wealth than others. The goal is not amassing wealth at all, let alone amassing more than your neighbor. I am not even sure "wealth" is in the alien dictionary, unless it refers to wealth of knowledge. There is no greed to gain more for yourself than you will need, while others suffer with less. That act alone, is totally based in ego and serves no productive purpose in alien culture.

If so, then how do aliens live, and pay their bills, and go on nice vacations, do you ask? The answer is that aliens would have all of their needs met by society. Obviously. Can you imagine an alien society purposely letting someone go hungry and homeless? That would be absurd and blasphemous. Remember, alien society is aimed at total cooperation toward technological and research advancement. They use every individual as a resource in achieving that end. Therefore, no individuals within their society are expendable or discarded. They find a function for everyone, and everyone has what they need to perform their function.

This means everyone has a home, food, equipment, and whatever else they need. This would include adequate rest and leisure time so that they may perform at their very best. Aliens value efficiency as an absolute requirement, and efficiency would call for making sure all of their individuals are in good health, rested, and have the physical and mental strength to perform their tasks and functions to the best of their ability.

For those of you starting to roll your eyes that I am outlining some kind of utopia agenda, no I am not. I am simply outlining a society that is based upon the three basic principles originally listed. You are free to disagree with the three principles if you would like, but given the observational evidence we have of aliens, those three principles are very reasonable assumptions that align with common sense and logic. So yes, those three principles would result in a more utopian society as compared to Earth. And I am not done yet.

Obviously, a major element in alien society is going to be EDUCATION. They likely begin to educate their children starting shortly after birth. They would have motor development exercises for baby aliens to develop basic thought and motor skills more quickly. Young children would be taught basic thought skills, reasoning skills, and diagnostic skills. Since technology is such an important part of their culture, most education would be focused on math, science, and logical problem solving. A typical final exam of an older child would likely be for them to solve a complicated problem, or to invent some kind of new device or method.

But let's not forget that technology is only one of the important cultural goals of aliens. Another is research. Therefore, their educational system would have very heavy instruction within the disciplines of History and Social Studies. No, they do not call them that, but you understand what those are. It would be important for young aliens to understand the cultures and worlds of those species and places they visit, focus on, and study. Earth Sciences and Human Society would most definitely be major required areas of instruction.

History would also be very important to them. They would study the history of their own species and worlds so that they can understand where they have been, where they are at, and why they are trying to go where they are going. History provides depth and context for why we do the things we do, and why we must never do certain things we have done in the past that didn't go well. Learning History can keep us all out of trouble in the present and future.

Education within the alien society is likely the most important priority of all. Not only would it be required for every soul, but it would be encouraged, and obviously provided without cost to every individual, from infants, all the way to the most advanced studies done by the oldest adults. To somehow discourage education by charging money, or making it difficult to access, would be unthinkable in an alien society. How is it logical to limit access to education? It's actually logical to make education so accessible that every individual will seek it and pursue it for as long as possible to the full extent of their potential. So yes, I believe an individual could study their entire life for free in an alien society. The society would find a way to make that individual's vast knowledge beneficial to the rest of society.

Relationships would be based upon mutual benefit, respect, cooperation, and efficiency. This would apply to personal relationships as well as professional ones. Remember, alien society is not based upon emotions, it is based upon logic. Thus, alien relationships would also be based upon logic instead of emotion. An alien likely doesn't understand love the same way humans do. Aliens care for each other and their children, as well as their culture, missions, and dreams. But aliens would not engage in irrational acts of "love" like humans do. The whole point of "human love" is to show irrational behavior to your mate in order to prove your love, right? Humans say things like, "I would jump off a bridge for you, or run into a burning building for you." Aliens would never say that because those things are not logical actions to take. So, they don't love in the same way humans do, but do not mistake that for them not deeply caring about each other as their form of love.

Aliens likely follow established breeding protocols. There would be encouragement for the most ideal genetics to be combined in breeding, to hopefully yield the most advanced and desirable new lives. Especially if a particular society is based upon a starship, there would be limitations upon breeding, and the number of children that are feasible for that situation on a starship, for example. The society is not based upon emotional desires, but rather on logic and efficiency.

All of you who were rolling your eyes earlier, thinking I was just here to outline alien society as a utopia that is more advanced or desirable than human society can relax. Now it's your turn. Because yes, alien society would be lacking in basic freedoms that human society enjoys. Humans can do pretty much what they want no matter how irrational, ridiculous, and unproductive it may be. That is why human society is a hot mess. "Freedom" is not "efficient." That is why there are some cultures and political structures on Earth that are more authoritarian in nature. Some in those cultures, especially the self-appointed authoritarian leaders, claim that it is more efficient and beneficial to have a strong, streamlined, and consistent government. Thus, they espouse the idea of trading political freedoms in favor of a more efficient and stronger government. But with that said, human society is fairly free for the most part, except for certain political constraints placed upon some regions of Earth as mentioned. Not to contradict myself, but let me also contradict myself by saying that humans are not nearly as free as they would like to think. Political, economic, and social structures heavily restrict human "freedom." But again, this might be a topic for a different book.

Very generally speaking, if you want a society more based on freedom as a guiding principle, then human society is where you want to look. If you want a more efficient, logical, and productive society, then alien society is where you want to look. I like to view alien society as "science," while human society is "art." Human society is like art because it is full of unexpected, irrational, thought and emotionally provoking expressions of emotion and freedom. Like art, human society is interesting. It allows for each individual to express themselves in very unique and individual ways.

Meanwhile, alien society is very disciplined and based upon efficiencies and proven procedures. Like science. Alien society pretty much guarantees productive successful outcomes because it is based upon proven Universal truths that work. Logic works. Following science works. But by thinking and living that way, there is no art. There is no freedom of unique expression that is unproductive. There is no rush of dating and love, and choosing your partner based upon irrational but exciting feelings and emotions that just seem "right." There is no art. A society without art. How sad would that be?

This brings us back to the discussion of the alien agenda. Aliens understand what I just described. They fully believe their way is better because it results in, well, better results. BUT aliens have seen the sparkle in the eyes of humans who revel in the joy of being human. They have seen the inner satisfaction of humans who find the right partner, or experience irrational things that give them a greater joy than an alien can experience. Aliens have seen how being unproductive can also be fun. This is a paradox for them, but they recognize the benefits and are intrigued.

Therefore, it is well worth their research time and resources to see if they can figure out how to introduce some of this "humanity" and "art" into their own very productive, efficient, and advanced society. Can it be done? Well, if anyone can figure it out, aliens can. Or, perhaps it is humans that can figure it out first, if humans are able to evolve in a direction more toward logic, efficiency, and advancement, while still retaining their humanity. Maybe the answer is that both species will meet in the middle at the same place. Perhaps

122

both species will seek the same balance. Imagine if both species worked together for this end. Well, that is up to them and to you.

CHAPTER FOURTEEN
Alien And Human Cohabitation

Will aliens and humans eventually cohabitate? Meaning, will aliens eventually live openly on Earth among humans? That is sort of a trick question because I believe it is already happening to some degree. But I wanted to explore the concept of aliens in non-human form living on Earth as part of our society.

Let's say one type of alien living among us were part of "The Greys," and thus were little grey beings with those big eyes. In other words, they would clearly be identified as aliens and stick out like a sore thumb. Could this be possible? Would it work out okay? How would you feel about that?

How about we take a look at current human society first. Humanity currently exists of many different races. One species, but many races, colors, shapes, and appearances. If you fill a room with ten humans and nine are small white women, and one is a large black man, that one male black person really stands out. If you fill a room with ten humans and nine of them are large black men and one is a small white woman, that one white woman really stands out.

In each of the two scenarios above, how does that make humans feel? The answer to that depends upon each person in the room of course. But some would feel very uncomfortable, while others would feel completely comfortable. Why? Well, that would depend upon each person's experience with multicultural groups. Humans who have experience living in a diverse community with many different races and types of people, tend to feel very comfortable with different races. Those who have only lived with people of their same race tend to be uncomfortable when mixed with other races.

Now let me contradict that premise above. If you put little children of different races together, they tend to have little problem functioning in a multi-race group. Why is that? Well clearly, there is something that happens between the time a human is a little child, and to when a human becomes a young man or woman. Somewhere during their upbringing, they are conditioned to feel comfortable or uncomfortable around those who are different than them. That is because human society is not totally comfortable with multi-race or multicultural societies. I do not think this is true in all areas around Earth. But it is certainly true in some countries and societies.

So, if humans have difficulty co-existing with different races of their own species, then how do you think humans would do co-existing with beings from a totally different species? Judging by how humans treat each other based upon race, color, sexuality, gender, and so forth, it is mind boggling and disturbing to imagine how humans would treat beings of a totally different species.

Would humans refuse to stand next to aliens? Refuse to eat with them? Refuse to allow them in schools, gyms, and restaurants? Would humans mock aliens by calling them derogatory names and picking on the unique features of aliens, such as a large head, large eyes, or grey skin color? You can imagine for yourself the possible hateful behavior that humans might inflict upon aliens, simply based upon the hateful behavior that humans inflict upon each other.

Why do humans behave this way? I think I already answered that, but sometimes it provides clarity to come full circle on things. As I previously mentioned, humans are often very uncomfortable with others different from them if they have had no positive conditioning or experience with others who are different from them. Humans feel fear and awkwardness toward others different from them, and they tend to react by belittling those different from them. It is like a human instinctual reflex action and coping mechanism.

It might appear that this chapter is going nowhere fast. The question was whether or not aliens would live openly among humans eventually. I think we have determined very quickly that this would be a huge problem. Humans do not currently have the maturity or ability to live openly with aliens, without inflicting undue harm and insult upon the aliens.

But could aliens live among humans on Earth from THEIR perspective? Assuming our environmental conditions are acceptable for long-term alien existence, I think aliens could live among humans, but perhaps with their own drawbacks. For example, imagine the patience required for a highly intelligent logical alien having to co-exist with humans who act in an illogical, irrational, unpredictable, and even hysterical way at times. Aliens might find humans too distasteful and might be unable to maintain the patience required to cope with such an existence.

Alright. So we have two different groups of beings who are very different, and perhaps even opposite in their nature and behaviors. Does this mean these two beings cannot co-exist? As cynical as I am about many things, I am very openly optimistic about the ability for different groups of people and beings to get along if they make the effort to find common ground. I speak about this quite a lot in my book EVOLVE. Humans can find a commonality among each other, and use that to build a positive mutually beneficial and enjoyable relationship, despite huge differences in opinions or cultures.

I believe the same concepts can be applied to developing relationships between humans and aliens. The first step in doing this would be to think of what humans and aliens might have in common. Of course, there might end up being many things, including things we cannot even imagine until humans and aliens meet and become acquainted. But let me suggest one item for discussion's sake.

I believe humans and aliens are both curious. Both species are very curious about things they know nothing about, and places they have never been. Both species are curious enough to both engage in space travel. While it is true that aliens face curiosity with logic, and humans face it with fear, the fact remains that both species are very curious and like to delve into the unknown.

Imagine the conversations humans and aliens could have about interesting places, things, and experiences, that one or the other has never had or imagined. For example, imagine the stories aliens could tell about planets they may have visited. Likewise, imagine what it might be like for aliens to listen to a human explain what it is like to sled down a hill of snow with good friends. Or what it is like to sit around a campfire telling ghost stories and eating toasted marshmallows. Or what it's like to fall in love and make love. There are many common human experiences that humans take for granted that would be entirely fascinating to aliens who may not ever experience such things in their culture.

I believe the differences between the two species would actually initiate amazing and powerful connections of conversation and sharing. Humans are completely fascinated with fantasy and adventure. Aliens have likely lived fantasy and adventure every day of their lives. Aliens are fascinated with the very deep and rich human connections of emotions. Humans live this daily and have plenty to offer in this area. Thus, the difference between the species is actually the catalyst for powerful bonding experiences by sharing stories that both species are captivated by.

Now let me ask the question again. Do you think humans and aliens could cohabitate together here on Earth? Perhaps the answer has changed. I will let you think about it, as the answer to this question is in the eye of the beholder.

Now let's flip the script. Do you think humans and aliens could cohabitate with the humans living within the alien's environment? Let's assume that the alien environment could support human life and there was adequate food and basic needs for human life. Let us assume that the alien environment was a huge starship, but of course it could also be a far-away planet.

Could humans live and thrive among an all-alien society? It would depend on the humans involved of course. Humans who have never been conditioned to accept different cultures and environments would not adjust well and likely could not do it. But humans who are very conditioned and open to different cultures, races, and environments, would likely do very well in an alien society.

It might be rough and a tough adjustment, but humans DO HAVE an incredible ability to adapt when they are forced to do so. They might not like change or adapting, but humans can, and often do, adjust and bend to new conditions and circumstances surrounding them. I believe plenty of humans could adjust and exist in an alien society. But let us hope that aliens would treat humans better than humans would treat aliens. I think they would. Aliens do not react out of fear, or lash out as a result of fear. Aliens will tend to be more logical and curious, and perhaps keep their own thoughts to themselves. Humans should definitely get used to being stared at though.

Let us continue our little journey of examination about the co-existence of aliens and humans. Let's assume that we managed to have aliens living with humans on Earth, and humans living with aliens up in space. What then? Well, what comes next is a wonderful, beautiful, and very productive sharing and synergy between two different species. Each species would be learning from the other. This would result in both species becoming more knowledgeable about life and all that surrounds them.

We would have the power of diversity making its magic, and causing the potential for great improvements and advancements in the societies of both species. When you have different species or cultures learning from each other, it makes BOTH species and cultures stronger and better. However different each culture is from each other, and however much they do not understand and don't agree with each other on certain things, they still both become much stronger and more advanced by having learned from each other.

I believe the alien culture would be very enriched by having learned the deep emotional connections that humans make with each other, and how they express those within their traditions, routines, and societies. Aliens would likely learn that logic is smart and efficient, but emotion is deep and enriching.

I feel that humanity would be very enriched by having learned the very advanced ways in which aliens think, reason, and work together in order to achieve things that humans cannot even imagine or dream about. Humans would realize that thinking and working together yields much better results than fighting and resisting against each other with irrational thinking.

So yes, I think both humans and aliens could cohabitate together. I think they could co-exist on Earth, and I think they could co-exist on an alien starship or alien planet. However, for this to happen there will have to be some giant leaps of maturity in how humans treat and interact with, those who are different from them. But I think the effort will be worth it. I think humans evolving into a species that can live peacefully with other species would be a major step in evolution to guarantee the long-term survival of humanity. Broadening your diversity and expanding your wisdom, understanding, and knowledge of the Universe, is a big step for any human, but a giant leap for humanity.

CHAPTER FIFTEEN
What's Next?

I shared my own personal experiences with you. I shared the opinions, theories, and knowledge I have been given by my own experiences, and by the consciousness in my head. I have presented my thoughts in a way that hopefully allows you to contemplate your own opinions and theories with more context and depth. Most of all, I have tried to guide our discussions in a way that might be useful in your own personal life going forward as you navigate society and personally evolve. You may have noticed that this book is just as much about humans as it is about aliens, perhaps even more so. That was by design. It is one thing to stipulate and pontificate about a subject such as aliens, for which there is not much absolute evidential proof, but it is another thing to do it in a way that is truly meaningful and helpful to humans in their daily realities of life. Most of my books and my client work focuses on helping people make their lives better. Thus, it is only natural I would be trying to do that here as well, even within a book about aliens.

But just as I was trying to do in my memoir, *The Walk-In*, I am also trying to de-stigmatize the topic of aliens, abductions, and other supernatural and paranormal events. Maybe if I share my experiences that are embarrassing, outlandish, or socially unacceptable, other people can feel they are not alone. I am not the only person who has experienced crazy things that seem unbelievable. I believe a huge percentage of the population has experienced something that is labeled as unbelievable. Whether it be a close encounter with an alien, ghost, entity, or perhaps some medical or mental event that was too real to only be a dream, or perhaps some other actual events that are too far beyond everyone's comprehension to be discussed, these things are real to those who experienced them.

Most people cannot publish their experiences publicly, such as in books, because they cannot risk being shunned socially, or having it affect them financially through their careers, businesses, and jobs. Some people treasure their religious faith, and know they cannot admit to their experiences without there being negative consequences within their faith community. Many people do not want to face the disapproval, criticism, or rejection of relationship partners or family members. Nobody wants to be an outcast in their community or society. Nobody wants to be looked down upon as crazy. So, people remain silent even though it would be healthier if they could share their experiences openly with others.

When it comes to the subject of aliens or anything supernatural and paranormal in nature, we have believers and we have non-believers. Why the difference? Why are some people able to accept such possibility, while others absolutely refuse to even consider the possibility?

I think the biggest factor would be between those who have personally experienced paranormal events, as opposed to those who have not. The best way to turn a non-believer into a believer, is by waiting for them to personally have a paranormal experience. Once you have experienced something crazy, you fully realize that "crazy" is possible and real. It does not matter how ridiculous the circumstances or the story, seeing is believing.

I grew up as a very grounded child in a wholesome rural area. I worked hard in school and worked hard outside of school as well. I learned to believe in FACTS, evidence, math, science, and to listen carefully when someone spoke in case there were contradictions. I did not think much about aliens or flying saucers. I don't think I cared whether they existed or not. I did not give psychic abilities much thought either, even though I can see now that I possessed such abilities at the time. With all that said, I would have called myself a Skeptic.

I was cynical of crazy stories that were not grounded in facts and logic that I could not relate to personally, or connect to science that I learned in school. If someone told me back then that they saw an alien spacecraft, I would have immediately thought they were crazy. I would not have said anything to their face, and I would have listened politely, but I would have walked away thinking that something was not quite right with them.

Basically, I would have called myself a non-believer, although with an open mind, and remained polite to those who thought differently. But of course, everything changed for me when I started to have my own experiences that I could not explain. I did not want to have any of those experiences. I did not ask for them, wish for them, and likely my life would have gone smoother without those experiences. But I went through what I went through, saw what I saw, and experienced what I experienced. It is what it is. I would be equally considered crazy if I were to live in denial and not acknowledge and accept my experiences. Insanity is not recognizing reality. I would have been insane if I refused to recognize the reality of my experiences. My reality is that weird, crazy, unexplained, paranormal, and supernatural things happened to me.

Even if it is inconvenient and uncomfortable, I had to own those experiences and events. This means also incurring the wrath, criticism, and consequences of doing so. I know there are plenty of non-believers who simply don't and can't believe in anything that seems crazy or weird. I know they cannot and will not believe me. I have to respect that. I am fine with that. I am actually fine with you not believing a single thing I have said in this book. I did not write this book to convince you of anything. I don't intend to have this book serve as any kind of proof of anything I have discussed. I am not under any illusions.

Again, I wrote this book to contribute my experiences, thoughts, theories, and knowledge, onto the pile of existing evidence and theories that already exist. I am speaking out as others have spoken out before me. I am doing so in my own voice with my own theories and ideas.

I have also done this in the hopes that others might feel more comfortable also speaking up, and speaking out by sharing experiences that have happened to them. By doing this, we begin to remove the stigma of people experiencing such events. These experiences will go from being totally crazy and false, to being considered legitimate and real if more people feel free to share their experiences.

Once we reach a certain level of societal acceptance, we can then move forward together as a society in researching and exploring all of our experiences in a more serious, collaborative, and cooperative way. When that begins to happen, we will begin to see humans evolve toward understanding, preparing, and accepting the eventual contact and interaction with aliens and other paranormal phenomena.

Now speaking in a different tone more professionally, I feel it is important for humans to begin evolving to a point that enables them to handle present and future contact with aliens. The key transition that humans must eventually make is transitioning from a FEAR-BASED way of thinking, to a more LOGIC-BASED way of thinking.

I am trying not to say it like it's a bad thing, but humans live under a totally fear-based psychology. What humans don't understand, they fear. What humans are not accustomed to, they fear. Anything humans are not knowledgeable of or comfortable with, they fear. Fear is always the default. It is a natural response for humans.

The problem with fear is that it makes humans do irrational, unproductive, and destructive things. Fear paralyzes us when we should be acting. Fear causes us to run when we should stand still. Fear causes us to lash out with violence when we should remain calm. Fear always makes us do the wrong thing.

Fear also blocks off all clear thought in our minds, and all clear feelings in our heart. Fear causes us pain inside. Fear is the moral enemy of humans. If God granted humans the blessings of love, emotion, and sensation, God also cursed humans with fear. God would have then said, "Let's see how they sort that out."

The human challenge is to embrace and leverage all of the best attributes given, and to evolve above all of the worst attributes humans have, such as fear and greed being the two largest. Maybe we can make the next book more about greed. But it's hard to talk about greed without getting political. I do not wish to get political. I am interested in helping humans become the best they can be. That is not political. Politics divides humans. Fear destroys humans. Fear is something all humans should be able to agree has to remain in check, totally controlled so that it does not control them.

The anti-force to fear is logic. While fear is based upon irrational emotion, logic is based upon clear intellect. Logic means always doing the rational correct thing regardless of your impulsive emotions of the moment. Logic is seeing reality for what it is, as clearly as possible.

Humans are fully capable of operating under logic. Scientists do it every day. Scientists do research based upon logical steps, testing, and outcomes, rather than just doing things they know will give them what they want. Yes, maybe some scientists do the latter, but they are not true scientists. A true scientist will do research with total attention to a legitimate process, and then let the outcome be whatever it shall be. Airplane pilots are also taught to think with logic. Pilots are taught to never panic, but to instead use lists, think clearly, and trust the instruments. Those are all very logical things, instead of submitting to fear, panic, and mistakes.

Thinking and acting with logic while maintaining your feelings, emotions, and compassion, is the definition of an evolved human in my humble opinion. Am I just lecturing and pontificating at this point? I am just rambling because I don't want this book to end? No,

134

there is actually a point to this exercise.

The point is that I believe the best way for humans to be prepared for a successful interaction with aliens, is to evolve to a point where they can better understand how an alien thinks and operates. Aliens are very logical, sophisticated, intelligent, advanced beings. If humans can relate to this better, then humans have a better chance of interacting with aliens peacefully, productively, and successfully.

I promise you that if humans react to aliens out of fear, it won't go well and it won't end well. You can take that as a dire warning, or you can take that as an encouragement to evolve and advance into a better state of mind and thinking.

And if you do not believe in aliens, or believe they are here, or are coming at all, then this evolution from fear into logic will still serve you well. By making this evolution, you will become a better, more competitive, more successful person in your life. So really, this suggestion of evolution I am making does not depend on aliens being real, nor does it need to have anything to do with aliens at all. It's a win-win.

Because of the benefits to humans and humanity, I wrote my book called *EVOLVE*, as a guide to help people make personal transformations to more advanced powerful people. Yes, I also discuss in *EVOLVE* how to develop advanced abilities, such as psychic abilities, more advanced communication, and I outline how I see a "first contact" situation with aliens happening. But most of the book is really about people's every day struggles and how to move beyond those into a more evolved and advanced person.

If you are a Believer, then the best thing you can do is prepare for further alien engagements. If you are a non-believer, then the best thing you can do is invest in yourself to continue improving and advancing your intellect and skills as a human, so that you can become more successful and happy within your life. It is not an accident that the perspectives and actions I have given for both Believers and non-believers, will benefit both parties.

Whether or not you believe in aliens, what is most important is that you believe in yourself. Humans have incredible gifts, and frightening weaknesses. Challenge yourself to make any adjustment and changes necessary to become the person you want to be. I will not tell you what you should be, any more than I have told you what to think. You are human (some of you), and thus you have the free will to choose your destiny. Make good choices and choose wisely. At the end of the day, aliens or no aliens, we are left with each other to love and encourage. We can all work together for a better life no matter what the Universe, God, fate, or aliens decide to throw at us. Much love to you on your continued journey within this Universe and your own personal evolution.

ACKNOWLEDGMENTS

Thank you Sarah Delamere Hurding for your editorial assistance, encouragement, and endless support.

Thanks to all of my clients and benefactors who have supported my mission of helping people become greater, stronger, more self-empowered, and free of pain.

Also, by Brian Hunter

EVOLVE is a cutting-edge, unique, powerful, and practical personal transformation self-help improvement book, which examines human life and all of its issues from a unique futuristic approach with a touch of humor. A selection of topics include: healing from personal losses and traumas, coping with sadness and depression, moving past fear that others use to control, manipulate, and abuse you, clarity in thinking, advanced communication skills, evolving your relationships, exploring the meaning of life, how everything in the Universe is connected, developing your psychic ability, and a little discussion about aliens possibly living among us. Yes, there is everything, which is all directly tied back to your own personal life.

The Walk-In is Brian's dramatic memoir that takes you on a personal life-long journey, from childhood, through coming-of-age discoveries, successes, failures, and deep depressions and struggles. The book describes paranormal events, resulting in the development of psychic abilities. This book is a very raw and honest adventure, which is not for the faint of heart, as it includes illicit scenes and themes.

The Hunter Equation is a practical spirituality book covering many topics, including life after death, reincarnation theory, cycle of life and death, human and animal souls, destiny vs. free will, synchronicities, Karma, soul mates, twin flames, angels, alien life, the future of humans, and many more topics. This is also the original book to unveil and fully explain the Hunter Equation life tool, and why it is far more relevant and accurate than The Law of Attraction.

Surviving Life: Contemplations Of The Soul is a unique and powerful book full of compassion and empathy, which combines the issues of what hurts us the most, with thoughts and advice meant to empower us toward happiness and independence. *Surviving Life* is medicine for the soul. It guides us through our deepest pains and weaknesses, and leads us to a place of self-empowerment, inspiration, strength, and hope. The topics covered are raw, diverse, and very practical. *Surviving Life* includes many subjects, and answers many questions, such as, "What is your purpose on this planet," "When you think nobody loves you," "How can you feel good," as well as practical advice on battling depression, suicide, and figuring out who you truly are. *Surviving Life* is a practical and contemplative manual for people of all ages, and the perfect book for gifting to those who need guidance and love.

Heal Me is a powerful and touching book that will pull at your heartstrings, give you practical advice on overcoming a variety of life traumas, and will put you on the road to recovery and healing. *Heal Me* examines such issues as the death of a loved one, loss of a pet, suicide, anxiety, addiction, life failures, major life mistakes, broken relationships, abuse, sexual assault, self-esteem, living in a toxic world surrounded by toxic people, loneliness, and many other issues. This is a self-care book written in a very loving, practical, and informative way that you can gift to yourself, family, young people, and friends, as a gesture of love, support, and hope.

Rising To Greatness is a self-help book that takes you on a step-by-step transformation, from the ashes of being broken and lost, to the greatness of self-empowerment, accomplishment, and happiness. This book includes such topics as developing your sense of self, eliminating fear from your life, mastering your emotions, self-discipline and motivation, communication skills, and so much more.

Living A Meaningful Life is an epic book series, with numerous installments, that will change your life. We are all capable of doing extraordinary things. We must only decide within ourselves to BE extraordinary. The *Living A Meaning Life* book series is a powerful story, and journey, of one such 'family' who dared to be extraordinary. By looking past their own obstacles in life, and choosing to always 'do the right things,' they became extraordinary within themselves, and this resulted in them doing extraordinary things that changed the lives of everyone around them, and their community. The main characters must navigate life struggles, both

139

personal, and community oriented. They do so by 'doing the right things,' through exhibiting integrity, decency, generosity, and compassion. Life is never easy, people make mistakes, but there is nothing that can't be overcome when we have the courage to do what we know is correct and true within our soul.

Printed in Great Britain
by Amazon

32830199R00079